British Railways

LOCO

FIFTY-NINTH EDITION
2017

The complete guide to all
Locomotives which operate on
the national railway
and Eurotunnel networks

Robert Pritchard & Peter Hall

ISBN 978 1909 431 30 0

© 2016. Platform 5 Publishing Ltd, 52 Broadfield Road, Sheffield, S8 0XJ, England.

Printed in England by The Lavenham Press, Lavenham, Suffolk.

All rights reserved. No part of this publication may be reproduced in any form or transmitted in any form by any means electronic, mechanical, photocopying, recording or otherwise without the prior permission of the publisher.

CONTENTS

Provision of information 2
Updates 2
Britain's Railway System 3
Introduction 10
General Information 12
1. Diesel Locomotives 16
2. Electro-Diesel & Electric Locomotives 62
3. Eurotunnel Locomotives 71
4. Former BR locomotives in Industrial Service 82
5. Locomotives Awaiting Disposal 85
6. Locomotives exported for use abroad 86
7. Codes 90

PROVISION OF INFORMATION

This book has been compiled with care to be as accurate as possible, but some information is not easily available and the publisher cannot be held responsible for any errors or omissions. We would like to thank the companies and individuals who have been helpful in supplying information to us. The authors of this series of books are always pleased to receive notification of any inaccuracies that may be found, to enhance future editions. Please send comments to:

Robert Pritchard, Platform 5 Publishing Ltd, 52 Broadfield Road, Sheffield, S8 0XJ, England.

e-mail: robert.pritchard@platform5.com **Tel:** 0114 255 2625.

This book is updated to information received by 3 October 2016.

UPDATES

This book is updated to the Stock Changes given in **Today's Railways UK 179** (November 2016). The Platform 5 railway magazine "**Today's Railways UK**" publishes Stock Changes every month to update this book. The magazine also contains news and rolling stock information on the railways of Great Britain and Ireland and is published on the second Monday of every month. For further details of **Today's Railways UK**, please contact Platform 5 Publishing Ltd.

Front cover photograph: Aggregate Industries-liveried 59001 "YEOMAN ENDEAVOUR" passes West Brompton with the 12.50 Acton–Purley on 06/06/14. **Antony Guppy**

BRITAIN'S RAILWAY SYSTEM

INFRASTRUCTURE & OPERATION

Britain's national railway infrastructure is owned by a "not for dividend" company, Network Rail. In 2014 Network Rail was reclassified as a public sector company, being described by the Government as a "public sector arm's-length body of the Department for Transport".

Most stations and maintenance depots are leased to and operated by Train Operating Companies (TOCs), but some larger stations are under Network Rail control. The only exception is the infrastructure on the Isle of Wight: The Island Line franchise uniquely included maintenance of the infrastructure as well as the operation of passenger services. As Island Line is now part of the South West Trains franchise, both the infrastructure and trains are operated by South West Trains.

Trains are operated by TOCs over Network Rail tracks (the National Network), regulated by access agreements between the parties involved. In general, TOCs are responsible for the provision and maintenance of the locomotives, rolling stock and staff necessary for the direct operation of services, whilst Network Rail is responsible for the provision and maintenance of the infrastructure and also for staff to regulate the operation of services.

The Department for Transport (DfT) is the franchising authority for the national network, with Transport Scotland overseeing the award of the ScotRail franchise and the Welsh Government overseeing the Wales & Borders franchise jointly with the DfT. TOCs can take commercial risks, although some franchises are "management contracts", where ticket revenues pass directly to the DfT. Concessions (such as London Overground) see the operator paid a fee to run the service, usually within specified guidelines. Operators running a concession would not normally take commercial risks, although there are usually penalties and rewards in the contract.

During 2012 the letting of new franchises was suspended pending a review of the franchise system. The process restarted in 2013 but it is taking a number of years to catch-up and several franchises are receiving short-term extensions (or "Direct Awards") in the meantime.

DOMESTIC PASSENGER TRAIN OPERATORS

The majority of passenger trains are operated by TOCs on fixed-term franchises or concessions. Franchise expiry dates are shown in the list below:

Franchise
Caledonian Sleeper

Franchisee
Serco
(until 31 March 2030)

Trading Name
Caledonian Sleeper

This new franchise started in April 2015 when operation of the ScotRail and ScotRail Sleeper franchises was separated. Abellio won the ScotRail franchise and Serco the Caledonian Sleeper franchise. Caledonian Sleeper operates four trains nightly between London Euston and Scotland using locomotives hired from GBRf or DB Schenker. New CAF rolling stock will be introduced from 2018.

BRITAIN'S RAILWAY SYSTEM

Chiltern   Arriva (Deutsche Bahn)   **Chiltern Railways**
(until 31 December 2021)

Chiltern Railways operates a frequent service between London Marylebone, Banbury and Birmingham Snow Hill, with some peak trains extending to Kidderminster. There are also regular services from Marylebone to Stratford-upon-Avon and to Aylesbury Vale Parkway via Amersham (along the London Underground Metropolitan Line). A new route to Oxford Parkway was added to the franchise in autumn 2015, and this line will be extended to Oxford in late 2016. The fleet consists of DMUs of Classes 121 (used on the Princes Risborough–Aylesbury route), 165, 168 and 172 plus a number of locomotive-hauled rakes used on some of the Birmingham route trains, worked by Class 68s hired from DRS.

Cross-Country   Arriva (Deutsche Bahn)   **CrossCountry**
(until October 2019)
There is an option to extend the franchise by 1 year to October 2020.

CrossCountry operates a network of long distance services between Scotland, North-East England and Manchester to the South-West of England, Reading, Southampton, Bournemouth and Guildford, centred on Birmingham New Street. These trains are mainly formed of diesel Class 220/221 Voyagers, supplemented by a small number of HSTs on the NE–SW route. Inter-urban services also link Nottingham, Leicester and Stansted Airport with Birmingham and Cardiff. These use Class 170 DMUs.

Crossrail   MTR   **Crossrail**
(until 30 May 2023)
There is an option to extend the concession by 2 years to May 2025.

This is a new concession which started in May 2015. Initially Crossrail took over the Liverpool Street–Shenfield stopping service from Abellio Greater Anglia, using a fleet of Class 315 EMUs, with the service branded "TfL Rail". New Class 345 EMUs will be introduced on this route from spring 2017 and then from 2018–19 Crossrail will operate through new tunnels beneath central London, from Shenfield and Abbey Wood in the east to Reading and Heathrow Airport in the west.

East Midlands   Stagecoach Group   **East Midlands Trains**
(until 4 March 2018)
There is an option to extend the franchise by 1 year to March 2019.

EMT operates a mix of long distance high speed services on the Midland Main Line (MML), from London St Pancras to Sheffield (Leeds at peak times and some extensions to York/Scarborough) and Nottingham (plus peak-hour trains to Lincoln), and local and regional services ranging from the Norwich–Liverpool route to Nottingham–Skegness, Newark–Mansfield–Worksop, Nottingham–Matlock and Derby–Crewe. It also operates local services in Lincolnshire. Trains on the MML are worked by a fleet of Class 222 DMUs and nine HSTs, whilst the local and regional fleet consists of DMU Classes 153, 156 and 158.

Essex Thameside   National Express Group   **c2c**
(until 8 November 2029)
There is an option to extend the franchise by seven reporting periods to May 2030.

c2c operates an intensive, principally commuter, service from London Fenchurch Street to Southend and Shoeburyness via both Upminster and Tilbury. The fleet consists entirely of Class 357 EMUs, with six Class 387s due to arrive in late 2016. In 2014 c2c won the new 15-year franchise that promised to introduce 17 new 4-car EMUs from 2019.

BRITAIN'S RAILWAY SYSTEM 5

| **Greater Western** | First Group (until 1 April 2019) | **Great Western Railway** |

There is an option to extend the franchise by 1 year to April 2020.

Great Western Railway (until September 2015 branded as First Great Western) operates long distance trains from London Paddington to South Wales, the West Country and Worcester and Hereford. In addition there are frequent trains along the Thames Valley corridor to Newbury/Bedwyn and Oxford, plus local and regional trains throughout the South-West including the Cornish, Devon and Thames Valley branches, the Reading–Gatwick North Downs line and Cardiff–Portsmouth Harbour and Bristol–Weymouth regional routes. A fleet of 54 HSTs is used on the long-distance trains, with DMUs of Classes 165 and 166 used on the North Downs and Thames Valley routes and Class 180s used alongside HSTs on the Cotswold Line to Worcester and Hereford. Classes 143, 150, 153 and 158 are used on local and regional trains in the South-West. A small fleet of four Class 57s is maintained to principally work the overnight "Cornish Riviera" Sleeper service between London Paddington and Penzance.

| **Greater Anglia** | Abellio (Netherlands Railways) (until 15 October 2025) | **Abellio Greater Anglia** |

Abellio Greater Anglia operates main line trains between London Liverpool Street, Ipswich and Norwich and local trains across Norfolk, Suffolk and parts of Cambridgeshire. It also runs local and commuter services into London Liverpool Street from the Great Eastern (including Southend, Braintree and Clacton) and West Anglia (including Cambridge and Stansted Airport) routes. It operates a varied fleet of Class 90s with locomotive-hauled Mark 3 sets, DMUs of Classes 153, 156 and 170 and EMUs of Classes 317, 321, 360 and 379. Two locomotive-hauled sets, using Class 37s and 68s, are hired on a temporary basis for use on some trains between Norwich and Great Yarmouth/Lowestoft.

| **Integrated Kent** | Govia (Go-Ahead/Keolis) (until 24 June 2018) | **Southeastern** |

Southeastern operates all services in the South-East London suburbs, the whole of Kent and part of Sussex, which are primarily commuter services to London. It also operates domestic high speed trains on HS1 from London St Pancras to Ashford, Ramsgate, Dover and Faversham with additional peak services on other routes. EMUs of Classes 375, 376, 465 and 466 are used, along with Class 395s on the High Speed trains.

| **InterCity East Coast** | Stagecoach/Virgin Trains (until 31 March 2023) | **Virgin Trains East Coast** |

There is an option to extend the franchise by 1 year to March 2024.

Virgin Trains East Coast operates frequent long distance trains on the East Coast Main Line between London King's Cross, Leeds, York, Newcastle and Edinburgh, with less frequent services to Bradford, Harrogate, Skipton, Hull, Lincoln, Glasgow, Aberdeen and Inverness. A mixed fleet of Class 91s and 30 Mark 4 sets, and 15 HST sets, are used on these trains.

| **InterCity West Coast** | Virgin Rail Group (Virgin/Stagecoach Group) (until 31 March 2018) | **Virgin Trains** |

Virgin Trains operates long distance services along the West Coast Main Line from London Euston to Birmingham/Wolverhampton, Manchester, Liverpool and Glasgow using Class 390 Pendolino EMUs. It also operates Class 221 Voyagers on the Euston–Chester–Holyhead route, whilst a mixture of 221s and 390s are used on the Euston–Birmingham–Glasgow/Edinburgh route.

BRITAIN'S RAILWAY SYSTEM

London Rail   MTR/Arriva (Deutsche Bahn)   **London Overground**
(until 12 November 2016)

This is a Concession and is different from other rail franchises, as fares and service levels are set by Transport for London instead of by the DfT.

London Overground operates services on the Richmond–Stratford North London Line and the Willesden Junction–Clapham Junction West London Line, plus the East London Line from Highbury & Islington to New Cross and New Cross Gate, with extensions to Clapham Jn (via Denmark Hill), Crystal Palace and West Croydon. It also runs services from London Euston to Watford Junction. All these use Class 378 EMUs whilst Class 172 DMUs are used on the Gospel Oak–Barking route. London Overground also took over the operation of some suburban services from London Liverpool Street in 2015 – to Chingford, Enfield Town and Cheshunt. These use Class 315 and 317 EMUs.

Merseyrail Electrics   Serco/Abellio (Netherlands Railways)   **Merseyrail**
(until 19 July 2028)

Under the control of Merseytravel PTE instead of the DfT. Franchise reviewed every five years to fit in with the Merseyside Local Transport Plan.

Merseyrail operates services between Liverpool and Southport, Ormskirk, Kirkby, Hunts Cross, New Brighton, West Kirby, Chester and Ellesmere Port, using Class 507 and 508 EMUs.

Northern Rail   Arriva (Deutsche Bahn)   **Northern**
(until 31 March 2025)

There is an option to extend the franchise by 1 year to March 2026.

Northern, operated by Arriva since April 2016, operates a range of inter-urban, commuter and rural services throughout the North of England, including those around the cities of Leeds, Manchester, Sheffield, Liverpool and Newcastle. The network extends from Chathill in the north to Nottingham in the south, and Cleethorpes in the east to St Bees in the west. Long distance services include Leeds–Carlisle, Middlesbrough–Carlisle and York–Blackpool North. The operator uses a large fleet of DMUs of Classes 142, 144, 150, 153, 155, 156 and 158 plus EMU Classes 319, 321, 322, 323 and 333. Class 185s are hired from TransPennine Express for use on some services between Manchester Airport and Blackpool North/Barrow/Windermere. Two locomotive-hauled sets, with Class 37s, are hired from DRS for use on some trains between Carlisle and Barrow-in-Furness/Preston.

ScotRail   Abellio (Netherlands Railways)   **ScotRail**
(until 31 March 2022)

There is an option to extend the franchise by 3 years to March 2025.

ScotRail provides almost all passenger services within Scotland and also trains from Glasgow to Carlisle via Dumfries, some of which extend to Newcastle (jointly operated with Northern). The company operates a large fleet of DMUs of Classes 156, 158 and 170 and EMU Classes 314, 318, 320, 334 and 380. Two locomotive-hauled rakes are also used on Fife Circle commuter trains, hauled by Class 68s hired from DRS.

South Western   Stagecoach Group   **South West Trains**
(until June 2017)

South West Trains operates trains from London Waterloo to destinations across the South and South-West including Woking, Basingstoke, Southampton, Portsmouth, Salisbury, Exeter, Reading and Weymouth as well as suburban services from Waterloo. SWT also runs services between Ryde and Shanklin on the Isle of Wight, using former London Underground 1938 stock (Class 483s). The rest of the fleet consists of DMU Classes 158 and 159 and EMU Classes 444, 450, 455, 456 and 458. Class 707s will be introduced in 2017.

BRITAIN'S RAILWAY SYSTEM

Thameslink & Great Northern Govia (Go-Ahead/Keolis) **Govia Thameslink Railway**
(until 19 September 2021)
There is an option to extend the franchise by 2 years to September 2023.

Govia operates this franchise, the largest in the UK, as a management contract. The former Southern franchise was combined with Thameslink/Great Northern in 2015. GTR uses four brands within the franchise: "Thameslink" for trains between Bedford and Brighton via central London and also on the Sutton/Wimbledon loop using Class 319, 377, 387 and new 700 EMUs. Some trains continue into Southeastern territory to Sevenoaks, Orpington and Ashford. "Great Northern" comprises services from London King's Cross and Moorgate to Welwyn Garden City, Hertford North, Peterborough, Cambridge and Kings Lynn using Class 313, 317, 321, 365 and 387 EMUs. "Southern" operates predominantly commuter services between London, Surrey and Sussex and metro services in South London, as well as services along the South Coast between Southampton, Brighton, Hastings and Ashford, plus the cross-London service from South Croydon to Milton Keynes. Class 171 DMUs are used on Brighton–Ashford and London Bridge–Uckfield services, whilst all other services are in the hands of Class 313, 377 and 455 EMUs. Finally, the premium "Gatwick Express" operates non-stop trains between London Victoria, Gatwick Airport and Brighton using Class 387/2 EMUs.

Trans-Pennine Express First Group/Keolis **TransPennine Express**
(until 31 March 2023)
There is an option to extend the franchise by 2 years to March 2025.

TransPennine Express operates predominantly long distance inter-urban services linking major cities across the North of England, along with Edinburgh and Glasgow in Scotland. The main services are Manchester Airport/Manchester Piccadilly–Newcastle/Middlesbrough/Hull plus Liverpool–Scarborough and Liverpool–Newcastle along the North Trans-Pennine route via Huddersfield, Leeds and York, and Manchester Airport–Cleethorpes along the South Trans-Pennine route via Sheffield. TPE also operates Manchester Airport–Edinburgh/Glasgow. Services to Blackpool North/Barrow/Windermere are now operated by Northern, The fleet consists of Class 185 DMUs, plus Class 350 EMUs used on Manchester Airport–Scotland services.

Wales & Borders Arriva (Deutsche Bahn) **Arriva Trains Wales**
(until 14 October 2018)
The franchise agreement includes the provision for the term to be further extended by mutual agreement by up to five years beyond October 2018. Management of the franchise is devolved to the Welsh Government, but DfT is still the procuring authority.

Arriva Trains Wales operates a mix of long distance, regional and local services throughout Wales, including the Valley Lines network of lines around Cardiff, and also through services to the English border counties and to Manchester and Birmingham. The fleet consists of DMUs of Classes 142, 143, 150, 158 and 175 and two loco-hauled rakes: one used on a premium Welsh Government sponsored service on the Cardiff–Holyhead route, and one used between Manchester/Crewe and Holyhead (both are hauled by a Class 67).

West Midlands Govia (Go-Ahead/Keolis) **London Midland**
(until October 2017)

London Midland operates long distance and regional services from London Euston to Northampton and Birmingham/Crewe and also between Birmingham and Liverpool as well as local and regional services around Birmingham, including to Stratford-upon-Avon, Worcester, Hereford, Redditch and Shrewsbury. It also operates the Bedford–Bletchley and Watford Jn–St Albans Abbey branches. The fleet consists of DMU Classes 150, 153, 170 and 172 and EMU Classes 319, 323 and 350.

BRITAIN'S RAILWAY SYSTEM

The following operators run non-franchised services (* special summer services only):

Operator	Trading Name	Route
BAA	Heathrow Express	London Paddington–Heathrow Airport
Hull Trains (part of First)	Hull Trains	London King's Cross–Hull
Grand Central (part of Arriva)	Grand Central	London King's Cross–Sunderland/Bradford Interchange
North Yorkshire Moors Railway Enterprises	North Yorkshire Moors Railway	Pickering–Grosmont–Whitby/Battersby
West Coast Railway Company	West Coast Railway Company	Birmingham–Stratford-upon-Avon* Fort William–Mallaig* York–Settle–Carlisle*

INTERNATIONAL PASSENGER OPERATORS

Eurostar International operates passenger services between the UK and mainland Europe. The company, established in 2010, is jointly owned by SNCF (the national operator of France): 55%, SNCB (the national operator of Belgium): 5% and Patina Rail: 40%. Patina Rail is made up of Canadian-based Caisse de dépôt et placement du Québec (CDPG) and UK-based Hermes Infrastructure (owning 30% and 10% respectively). This 40% was previously owned by the UK Government until it was sold in 2015.

In addition, a service for the conveyance of accompanied road vehicles through the Channel Tunnel is provided by the tunnel operating company, Eurotunnel.

FREIGHT TRAIN OPERATORS

The following operators operate freight services or empty passenger stock workings under "Open Access" arrangements:

Colas Rail: Colas Rail operates a number of On-Track machines and also supplies infrastructure trains for Network Rail. It also now operates a number of different freight flows, including steel, coal, oil and timber. Colas Rail has a small but varied fleet consisting of Class 37s, 47s, 56s, 60s, 66s and 70s.

DB Cargo (UK): Still the biggest freight operator in the country, DBC (EWS until bought by Deutsche Bahn, when it was initially called DB Schenker) provides a large number of infrastructure trains to Network Rail and also operates coal, steel, intermodal and aggregate trains nationwide. The core fleet is Class 66s. Of the original 250 ordered some have moved to DB's French and Polish operations, although some of the French locos do return to the UK when major maintenance is required. A fleet of around 15–20 Class 60s are also used on heavier trains.

DBS's six Class 59/2s are used alongside the Mendip Rail 59/0s and 59/1s on stone traffic from the Mendip quarries and around the South-East. DBC's fleet of Class 67s are used on passenger or standby duties for Arriva Trains

BRITAIN'S RAILWAY SYSTEM 9

Wales and Virgin Trains East Coast and also on excursions or special trains. Class 90s see some use on West Coast Main Line freight traffic. The Class 92s are used on a limited number of overnight freights on High Speed 1.

DBS also operates the Class 325 EMUs for Royal Mail and a number of excursion trains.

Devon & Cornwall Railways (a subsidiary of British American Railway Services): DCRail specialises in short-term freight haulage contracts, mainly in the scrap, coal and aggregates markets, using its fleet of Class 56s. It also provides locomotives from its fleet of Class 31s or 56s for stock moves or to move On-Track Machines or other equipment.

Direct Rail Services: DRS has built on its original nuclear flask traffic to operate a number of different services. The main flows are intermodal plus the provision of crews and locomotives to Network Rail for autumn Railhead Treatment Trains and also operates some NR infrastructure trains. Its Class 57s and 68s are used on excursion work.

DRS has a varied fleet of locomotives, with Class 20s, 37s, 57s and 66s working alongside new Class 68s that are currently being delivered. The company has 32 Class 68s on order as well as ten new Vossloh electric locomotives (Class 88s), that will feature a small diesel engine.

Freightliner: Freightliner has two divisions: Intermodal operates container trains from the main Ports at Southampton, Felixstowe, Tilbury and Thamesport to major cities including London, Manchester, Leeds and Birmingham. The Heavy Haul division covers the movement of coal, cement, infrastructure and aggregates nationwide. Most services are worked by Class 66s, with Class 70s mainly used on some of the heavier intermodal trains. A small fleet of Class 86 and 90 electrics is used on intermodal trains on the Great Eastern and West Coast Main Lines, the Class 86s mainly being used in pairs on the WCML between Crewe and Coatbridge. Class 90s are also hired to Caledonian Sleeper.

GB Railfreight: GBRf, owned by Eurotunnel, operates a mixture of traffic types, mainly using Class 66s together with a small fleet of Class 73s on infrastructure duties and test trains in the South-East. A growing fleet of Class 92s is also used on some intermodal flows to/from Dollands Moor or through the Channel Tunnel to Calais. Traffic includes coal, intermodal, biomass, aggregates and gypsum as well as infrastructure services for Network Rail and London Underground. GBRf also supplies locomotives to Caledonian Sleeper.

GBRf also operates some excursion trains, including those using the preserved Class 201 "Hastings" DEMU.

Rail Operations Group: This company mainly facilitates rolling stock movements by providing drivers or using locomotives hired from other companies or by using its own fleet of Class 47s.

West Coast Railway Company: WCRC has a freight licence but doesn't operate any freight as such – only empty stock movements. Its fleet of Class 47s, supplemented by a smaller number of Class 33s, 37s and 57s, is used on excursion work nationwide.

In addition Amey, Balfour Beatty Rail, Harsco Rail, South West Trains, Swietelsky Babcock Rail (SB Rail) and VolkerRail operate trains formed of On-Track Machines.

INTRODUCTION

This book contains details of all locomotives which can run on Britain's national railway network, plus those of Eurotunnel.

Locomotives currently approved for use on the national railway network fall into the four broad types: passenger, freight, mixed traffic and shunting.

Passenger
The number of dedicated passenger locomotives has not changed significantly in recent years. However, the number is expected to decline in the future as new multiple unit stock replaces some of the remaining locomotive-hauled or propelled trains. Classes 43 (HST) and 91 and some members of Classes 57, 67, 68, 73/9, 90 and 92 are dedicated to franchised and Open Access passenger operations. Excursion trains have a few dedicated locomotives but mainly use locomotives that are best described as mixed traffic.

Freight
By far the most numerous locomotives are those used solely for bulk commodity and intermodal freight. Since 1998 a large number of new Class 66 locomotives have replaced many former BR designs and in more recent years smaller numbers of Class 70s have also been introduced. There are however a significant number of BR era Class 20, 37, 47, 56, 60, 73/1, 86, 90 and 92 locomotives still in use; their number has increased slightly recently as some locomotives have been reinstated to cope with demand. In addition there is a small fleet of Class 59s acquired privately in the 1980s and 1990s and a small number of re-engined Class 57s in use.

Mixed Traffic
In addition to their use on passenger and commodity freight workings these locomotives are used for stock movements and specialist infrastructure and test trains. The majority, but not all, are fitted with Electric Train Supply. Locomotives from Classes 20, 31, 33, 37, 47, 57, 67, 68, 73/9 and 90 fall into this category. Also included under this heading are preserved locomotives permitted to operate on the national railway network. Although these have in the past solely operated excursion trains they are increasingly seeing occasional use on other types of trains.

Shunting
Very few shunting locomotives are now permitted to operate freely on the National Railway network. The small number that are have to be fitted with a plethora of safety equipment in order to have engineering acceptance. They are mainly used for local workings such as trips between yards or stock movements between depots and stations. In the main section of this book all such shunting locomotives (Classes 08 and 09) in the fleets that have permitted locomotives are included. Otherwise, shunting locomotives are not permitted to venture from depots or yards onto the National Railway network other than into defined limits within interface infrastructure. Generally such locomotives, which include an increasing number of remotely controlled driverless types, are not included in this book. However, those of BR pedigree, such as Class 08s, can be found in Section 4 – Former BR Locomotives in Industrial Service.

INTRODUCTION

Locomotives which are owned by, for example, DB Cargo or Freightliner, which have been withdrawn from service and are awaiting disposal are listed in the main part of the book. Locomotives which are awaiting disposal at scrapyards are listed in the "Locomotives Awaiting Disposal" section.

Only preserved locomotives which are currently used on the National Railway network are included. Others, which may still be Network Rail registered but not at present certified for use, are not included, but can be found in the Platform 5 book, "Preserved Locomotives of British Railways".

LAYOUT OF INFORMATION

Locomotive classes are listed in numerical order of class. Principal details and dimensions are quoted for each class in metric and/or imperial units as considered appropriate bearing in mind common UK usage.

Where numbers actually carried are different from those officially allocated, these are noted in class headings where appropriate. Where locomotives have been recently renumbered, the most immediate previous number is shown in parentheses. Each locomotive entry is laid out as in the following example:

No.   Detail Livery Owner Pool   Allocn.   Name

59206 *b   **DB**   DB   WDAM   MD   John F. Yeoman Rail Pioneer

Detail Differences. Only detail differences which currently affect the areas and types of train which locomotives may work are shown. All other detail differences are excluded. Where such differences occur within a class or part class, they are shown in the "Detail" column alongside the individual locomotive number.

Codes: Codes are used to denote the livery, owner, pool and depot of each locomotive. Details of these will be found in section 7 of this book.

Depot allocation codes for all locomotives are shown in this book (apart from shunting locomotives (Class 08 & 09) where the actual location of each is shown). It should be noted that today much locomotive maintenance is undertaken away from these depots. This may be undertaken at fuelling points, berthing sidings or similar, or by mobile maintenance teams. Therefore locomotives in particular may not return to their "home" depots as often as in the past.

(S) denotes that the locomotive is stored (the actual location is shown).

Names: Only names carried with official sanction are listed. Names are shown in UPPER/lower case characters as actually shown on the name carried on the locomotive.

GENERAL INFORMATION

CLASSIFICATION AND NUMBERING

All locomotives are classified and allocated numbers under the TOPS numbering system, introduced in 1972. This comprises a two-digit class number followed by a three-digit serial number.

For diesel locomotives, class numbers offer an indication of engine horsepower as shown in the table below.

Class No. Range	Engine hp
01–14	0–799
15–20	800–1000
21–31	1001–1499
32–39	1500–1999
40–54, 57	2000–2999
55–56, 58–70	3000+

For electric locomotives class numbers are allocated in ascending numerical order under the following scheme:

Class 71–80   Direct current and DC/diesel dual system locomotives.
Class 81 onwards   Alternating current and AC/DC dual system locomotives.

Numbers in the 89xxx series are allocated to locomotives which have been deregistered but subsequently re-registered for use on the national railway network and whose original number has already been reused. 89xxx numbers are normally only carried inside locomotive cabs and are not carried externally in normal circumstances.

WHEEL ARRANGEMENT

For main line locomotives the number of driven axles on a bogie or frame is denoted by a letter (A = 1, B = 2, C = 3 etc) and the number of non-powered axles is denoted by a number. The use of the letter "o" after a letter indicates each axle is individually powered, whilst the "+" symbol indicates bogies are inter-coupled.

For shunting locomotives, the Whyte notation is used. In this notation the number of leading wheels are given, followed by the number of driving wheels and then the trailing wheels.

UNITS OF MEASUREMENT

All dimensions and weights are quoted for locomotives in an "as new" condition with all necessary supplies (eg oil, water and sand) on board. Dimensions are quoted in the order length x width. Lengths quoted are over buffers or couplers as appropriate. All widths quoted are maxima. Where two different wheel diameter dimensions are shown, the first refers to powered wheels and the second refers to non-powered wheels. All weights are shown as metric tonnes (t = tonnes).

GENERAL INFORMATION

HAULAGE CAPABILITY OF DIESEL LOCOMOTIVES

The haulage capability of a diesel locomotive depends upon three basic factors:

1. Adhesive weight. The greater the weight on the driving wheels, the greater the adhesion and more tractive power can be applied before wheelslip occurs.

2. The characteristics of its transmission. To start a train the locomotive has to exert a pull at standstill. A direct drive diesel engine cannot do this, hence the need for transmission. This may be mechanical, hydraulic or electric. The present British Standard for locomotives is electric transmission. Here the diesel engine drives a generator or alternator and the current produced is fed to the traction motors. The force produced by each driven wheel depends on the current in its traction motor. In other words, the larger the current, the harder it pulls. As the locomotive speed increases, the current in the traction motor falls, hence the *Maximum Tractive Effort* is the maximum force at its wheels the locomotive can exert at a standstill. The electrical equipment cannot take such high currents for long without overheating. Hence the *Continuous Tractive Effort* is quoted which represents the current which the equipment can take continuously.

3. The power of its engine. Not all power reaches the rail, as electrical machines are approximately 90% efficient. As the electrical energy passes through two such machines (the generator or alternator and the traction motors), the *Power at Rail* is approximately 81% (90% of 90%) of the engine power, less a further amount used for auxiliary equipment such as radiator fans, traction motor blowers, air compressors, battery charging, cab heating, Electric Train Supply (ETS) etc. The power of the locomotive is proportional to the tractive effort times the speed. Hence when on full power there is a speed corresponding to the continuous tractive effort.

HAULAGE CAPABILITY OF ELECTRIC LOCOMOTIVES

Unlike a diesel locomotive, an electric locomotive does not develop its power on board and its performance is determined only by two factors, namely its weight and the characteristics of its electrical equipment. Whereas a diesel locomotive tends to be a constant power machine, the power of an electric locomotive varies considerably. Up to a certain speed it can produce virtually a constant tractive effort. Hence power rises with speed according to the formula given in section three above, until a maximum speed is reached at which tractive effort falls, such that the power also falls. Hence the power at the speed corresponding to the maximum tractive effort is lower than the maximum speed.

BRAKE FORCE

Brake Force (also known as brake power) is a measure of the braking power of a locomotive. The Brake Force available is dependant on the adhesion between the rail and the wheels being braked and the normal reaction of the rail on the wheels being braked (and hence on the weight per braked wheel). A locomotive's Brake Force is shown on its data panels so operating staff can ensure sufficient brake power is available for specific trains.

ELECTRIC TRAIN SUPPLY (ETS)

A number of locomotives are equipped to provide a supply of electricity to the train being hauled to power auxiliaries such as heating, cooling fans, air conditioning and kitchen equipment. ETS is provided from the locomotive by means of a separate alternator (except Class 33 locomotives, which have a DC generator). The ETS index of a locomotive is a measure of the electrical power available for train supply. Class 55 locomotives provide an ETS directly from one of their traction generators into the train supply.

Similarly, most locomotive-hauled carriages also have an ETS index, which in this case is a measure of the power required to operate equipment mounted in the carriage. The sum of the ETS indices of all the hauled vehicles in a train must not exceed the ETS index of the locomotive.

ETS is commonly (but incorrectly) known as ETH (Electric Train Heating), which is a throwback to the days before locomotive-hauled carriages were equipped with electrically powered auxiliary equipment other than for train heating.

ROUTE AVAILABILITY (RA)

This is a measure of a railway vehicle's axle load. The higher the axle load of a vehicle, the higher the RA number on a scale from 1 to 10. Each Network Rail route has a RA number and in general no vehicle with a higher RA number may travel on that route without special clearance.

MULTIPLE WORKING

Multiple working between vehicles (ie two or more powered vehicles being driven from one cab) is facilitated by jumper cables connecting the vehicles. However, not all types of locomotive are compatible with each other, and a number of different systems are in use. Some are compatible with others, some are not. BR used "multiple working codes" to designate which locomotives were compatible. The list below shows which classes of locomotives are compatible with each other – the former BR multiple working code being shown in brackets. It should be noted that some locomotives have had the equipment removed or made inoperable.

GENERAL INFORMATION 15

With other classes:
Classes 20, 25, 31, 33, 37 40 & 73/1*. (Blue Star)
Classes 56 & 58. (Red Diamond)
Classes 59, 66, 67, 68, 70 & 73/9.
* DRS has since adapted the systems so its Classes 20/3, 37, 47 & 57 can work with each other only.

With other members of same class only:
Class 43, Class 47 (Green Circle), Class 50 (Orange Square), Class 60.

PUSH-PULL OPERATION

Some locomotives are modified to operate passenger and service (formed of laboratory, test and inspection carriages) trains in "push-pull" mode – which allows the train to be driven from either end – either with locomotives at each end (both under power) or with a driving brake van at one end and a locomotive at the other. Various different systems are now in use. Electric locomotive Classes 86, 87, 90 & 91 use a time-division multiplex (TDM) system for push-pull working which utilises the existing Railway Clearing House (RCH) jumper cables fitted to carriages. Previously these cables had only been used to control train lighting and public address systems.

More recently locomotives of Classes 67 and 68 have used the Association of American Railroads (AAR) system.

ABBREVIATIONS

Standard abbreviations used in this book are:

a   Train air brake equipment only.
b   Drophead buckeye couplers.
c   Scharfenberg couplers.
d   Fitted with retractable Dellner couplers.
e   European Railway Traffic Management System (ERTMS) signalling equipment fitted.
k   Fitted with Swinghead Automatic "buckeye" combination couplers.
p   Train air, vacuum and electro-pneumatic brakes.
r   Radio Electric Token Block signalling equipment fitted.
s   Slow Speed Control equipment.
v   Train vacuum brake only.
x   Train air and vacuum brakes ("Dual brakes").
+   Additional fuel tank capacity.
§   Sandite laying equipment.

In all cases use of the above abbreviations indicates the equipment in question is normally operable. The definition of non-standard abbreviations and symbols is detailed in individual class headings.

1. DIESEL LOCOMOTIVES

CLASS 08   BR/ENGLISH ELECTRIC   0-6-0

Built: 1955–62 by BR at Crewe, Darlington, Derby Locomotive, Doncaster or Horwich Works.
Engine: English Electric 6KT of 298 kW (400 hp) at 680 rpm.
Main Generator: English Electric 801.
Traction Motors: Two English Electric 506.
Maximum Tractive Effort: 156 kN (35000 lbf).
Continuous Tractive Effort: 49 kN (11100 lbf) at 8.8 mph.
Power at Rail: 194 kW (260 hp).   **Train Brakes:** Air & vacuum.
Brake Force: 19 t.   **Dimensions:** 8.92 x 2.59 m.
Weight: 49.6–50.4 t.   **Wheel Diameter:** 1372 mm.
Design Speed: 20 mph.   **Maximum Speed:** 15 mph.
Fuel Capacity: 3037 litres.   **Route Availability:** 5.
Train Supply: Not equipped.

† – Fitted with remote control equipment.

For shunting locomotives, instead of the two-letter depot code, actual locations at the time of publication are given.

Locomotives of Classes 08 and 09 that don't have current Network Rail engineering acceptance and are considered to be "in industrial service" can be found in section 4 of this book.

08850 has acceptance for use between Battersby and Whitby only, for rescue purposes.

Non-standard liveries/numbering:

08480	Yellow with a red bodyside band. Carries number "TOTON No 1".
08605	Carries the number "WIGAN2".
08616	Carries the number 3783.
08899	Crimson lake.

Class 08/0. Standard Design.

08405	a†	**E**	DB	WQAA	Crewe International Depot (S)
08410	a	**GW**	GW	EFSH	Penzance Long Rock depot
08417	a	**Y**	NR	QADD	LORAM Derby
08428	ak	**E**	DB	WSSC	Warrington Yards
08451		**B**	AM	ATLO	Glasgow Polmadie Depot
08454		**K**	AM	ATLO	Arlington Fleet Services, Eastleigh Works
08472	a	**WA**	WA	RFSH	Edinburgh Craigentinny Depot
08480	a	**0**	DB	WQAB	Toton Depot (S)
08483	a	**K**	GW	EFSH	Old Oak Common HST Depot
08495	†	**E**	DB	WQBA	Crewe International Depot (S)
08523		**RS**	RL	MRSO	Inverness Depot
08525		**ST**	EM	EMSL	Leeds Neville Hill Depot
08530		**FL**	P	DFLS	Felixstowe FLT
08531	a	**FH**	P	DFLS	LH Group, Barton-under-Needwood

▲ GWR has painted its shunters into "retro" liveries. In InterCity livery, 08822 is seen at Bristol St Philip's Marsh depot on 02/05/16. **Robert Pritchard**

▲ GBRf-liveried 20905 and BR Blue 20096 lead a train of London Underground S-Stock past Syston South Junction with 7X23 09.19 Derby–Old Dalby on 26/08/16. **Paul Biggs**

▼ DCR Green-liveried 31452 passes Alsager hauling preserved 47712 and 47192 from Barrow Hill to Crewe on 13/04/16. **Cliff Beeton**

▲ West Coast Railway Company Maroon-liveried 33207 and 47237 pass Chaloners Whin, south of York, with a return Scarborough–Carnforth railtour on 08/09/16.
Sean White

▼ Europhoenix-liveried 37884 is seen at Bristol St Philip's Marsh depot on 02/05/16. **Robert Pritchard**

▲ Revised Direct Rail Services-liveried 37405 and 37422 top-and-tail the 12.36 Norwich–Great Yarmouth at Stacey Arms on 18/07/16. **Dave Gommersall**

▲ Stagecoach East Midlands Trains-liveried 43043 is seen at Nottingham on 17/07/16. **Robert Pritchard**

▼ Grand Central-liveried 43423 leads the 08.30 Sunderland–London King's Cross at Colton on 19/09/15. **Andrew Mason**

▲ Colas Rail-liveried 47739 passes Besford with 5V47 09.00 Washwood Heath–Cardiff Canton (hauling vans 6364 and 6365) on 16/05/16. **Raymond Coates**

▼ BR Blue-liveried 50007 and 50050 pass Banbury with a Pathfinder railtour from Derby to Swanage on 11/06/16. **James Martin**

▲ BR Maroon-liveried D1015 passes South Brent with a railtour from London Paddington to Okehampton on 07/05/16 . **Tony Christie**

▼ Colas Rail-liveried 56105 and 56087 top-and-tail 6Z47 11.54 York–Kings Norton at Barrow-upon-Trent on 30/09/15. **Steve Madden**

▲ Original Great Western Railway Green-liveried 57604 awaits departure from Exeter St Davids with the 17.50 to Penzance on 13/08/16. **David Hunt**

▼ GB Railfreight-liveried 59003 stands in Heeley loop, Sheffield with 6M83 10.51 Tinsley–Bardon Hill empty aggregates train on 31/08/16. **Chris Booth**

08571 a	**WA**	WA	HBSH	Felixstowe FLT
08575	**FL**	P	DHLT	LH Group, Barton-under-Needwood (S)
08585	**FL**	P	DFLS	Trafford Park FLT
08596 a†	**WA**	WA	HBSH	Edinburgh Craigentinny Depot
08605 †	**DB**	DB	WQBA	Wigan Springs Branch Depot
08611	**B**	AM	ATLO	Wembley Depot
08615	**WA**	WA	RFSH	LH Group, Barton-under-Needwood
08616	**LM**	LM	EJLO	Birmingham Tyseley Depot
08617	**B**	AM	ATLO	Arlington Fleet Services, Eastleigh Works
08623	**DB**	DB	WQBA	Bescot Yards (S)
08624	**FH**	P	DFLS	Felixstowe FLT
08632 †	**DB**	DB	WSRC	Mossend Yards
08633 †	**E**	DB	WQCA	Axiom Rail, Stoke-on-Trent Works
08641	**B**	GW	EFSH	Plymouth Laira Depot
08644	**B**	GW	EFSH	Plymouth Laira Depot
08645	**DG**	GW	EFSH	Plymouth Laira Depot
08663 a	**B**	GW	EFSH	Bristol St Philip's Marsh Depot
08669 a	**WA**	WA	RFSH	Wabtec Rail, Doncaster Works
08690	**ST**	EM	EMSL	Leeds Neville Hill Depot
08691	**FL**	FL	DFLS	Southampton Maritime FLT
08696 a	**B**	AM	ATLO	Wembley Depot
08703 a	**E**	DB	WSSC	Bescot Yards
08706 †	**E**	DB	WQCA	Crewe International Depot (S)
08721	**B**	AM	ATLO	Manchester Longsight Depot
08724	**WA**	WA	HBSH	Wabtec Rail, Doncaster Works
08735 †	**E**	DB	WQCA	Eastleigh Yards (S)
08742 †	**RX**	DB	WSSC	Hinksey Yard
08752 †	**E**	DB	WSSC	Bescot Yards
08754	**B**	RL	MRSO	Norwich Crown Point Depot
08757 †	**RG**	DB	WQBA	Crewe International Depot (S)
08764	**B**	AM	ATLO	Glasgow Polmadie Depot
08782 a†	**CU**	DB	WQBA	Doncaster Yards (S)
08784 †	**E**	DB	WQBA	Toton Depot (S)
08785 a	**FL**	P	DFLS	Southampton Maritime FLT
08788	**K**	RL	MRSO	Tata Steel, Shotton Works
08790	**B**	AM	ATLO	Wolverhampton Oxley Depot
08795	**K**	GW	EFSH	Swansea Landore Depot
08799 a	**E**	DB	WQAB	Westbury Yards (S)
08804 †	**E**	DB	WQBA	Crewe International Depot (S)
08805	**FO**	LM	EJLO	Birmingham Soho Depot
08822	**IC**	GW	EFSH	Bristol St Philip's Marsh Depot
08836	**GW**	GW	EFSH	Old Oak Common HST Depot
08847	**CD**	RL	MRSO	Norwich Crown Point Depot
08850	**B**	NY	MBDL	Grosmont Depot
08853 a	**WA**	WA	RFSH	Wabtec Rail, Doncaster Works
08874	**SL**	RL	MRSO	Tata Steel, Shotton Works
08879 †	**E**	DB	WQAB	Margam Yards (S)
08887 a	**B**	AM	ATLO	Arlington Fleet Services, Eastleigh Works
08888 †	**E**	DB	WSSC	Hoo Junction Yards
08891	**FL**	P	DHLT	LH Group, Barton-under-Needwood (S)
08899	**O**	EM	EMSL	Derby Etches Park Depot

08904	E	DB	WSGC	Eastleigh Yards
08907	**DB**	DB	WQBA	Bescot Yards (S)
08908	**ST**	EM	EMSL	Leeds Neville Hill Depot
08922	**DG**	DB	WQBA	Toton Depot (S)
08925	**G**	GB	GBWM	Barrow Hill Roundhouse
08934 a	**VP**	GB	GBWM	GBRf, Dagenham
08948 c	**EP**	EU	GPSS	Temple Mills Depot
08950	**ST**	EM	EMSL	Leeds Neville Hill Depot
08954	**B**	AM	ATLO	Liverpool Edge Hill Depot

Class 08 names:

08451	M.A. SMITH
08483	NEIL / SCOUSEY
	Neil Morgan 1964–2014
	Team Leader O.O.C.
08495	NOEL KIRTON OBE
08525	DUNCAN BEDFORD
08585	Vicky
08616	TYSELEY 100
08617	Steve Purser
08644	Laira Diesel Depot
	50 Years 1962–2012
08645	Mike Baggott
08663	St. Silas
08669	Bob Machin
08690	DAVID THIRKILL
08691	Terri
08721	Longsight TMD
08799	FRED
08822	Dave Mills
08874	Catherine
08899	Midland Counties Railway
	175 1839–2014
08908	IVAN STEPHENSON
08950	DAVID LIGHTFOOT

CLASS 09   BR/ENGLISH ELECTRIC   0-6-0

Built: 1959–62 by BR at Darlington or Horwich Works.
Engine: English Electric 6KT of 298 kW (400 hp) at 680 rpm.
Main Generator: English Electric 801.
Traction Motors: English Electric 506.
Maximum Tractive Effort: 111 kN (25000 lbf).
Continuous Tractive Effort: 39 kN (8800 lbf) at 11.6 mph.
Power at Rail: 201 kW (269 hp).   **Train Brakes:** Air & vacuum.
Brake Force: 19 t.   **Dimensions:** 8.92 x 2.59 m.
Weight: 49 t.   **Wheel Diameter:** 1372 mm.
Design Speed: 27 mph.   **Maximum Speed:** 27 mph.
Fuel Capacity: 3037 litres.   **Route Availability:** 5.
Train Supply: Not equipped.

Class 09/0. Built as Class 09.

09002	**G**	GB	GBWM	March Whitemoor Yard
09009	**G**	GB	GBWM	March Whitemoor Yard

Class 09/1. Converted from Class 08 1992–93 by RFS Industries, Kilnhurst.

09106 (08759)	**DB**	DB	WSGC	Knottingley Depot

CLASS 20   ENGLISH ELECTRIC   Bo-Bo

Built: 1957–68 by English Electric at Vulcan Foundry, Newton-le-Willows or by Robert Stephenson & Hawthorns at Darlington.
Engine: English Electric 8SVT Mk II of 746 kW (1000 hp) at 850 rpm.
Main Generator: English Electric 819/3C.
Traction Motors: English Electric 526/5D or 526/8D.
Maximum Tractive Effort: 187 kN (42000 lbf).
Continuous Tractive Effort: 111 kN (25000 lbf) at 11 mph.
Power at Rail: 574 kW (770 hp).   **Train Brakes:** Air & vacuum.
Brake Force: 35 t.   **Dimensions:** 14.25 x 2.67 m.
Weight: 73.4–73.5 t.   **Wheel Diameter:** 1092 mm.
Design Speed: 75 mph.   **Maximum Speed:** 75 mph.
Fuel Capacity: 1727 litres.   **Route Availability:** 5.
Train Supply: Not equipped.

Class 20s that don't have current Network Rail engineering acceptance and are considered to be "in industrial service" can be found in section 4 of this book.

Non-standard liveries/numbering:

20088 RFS grey (carries No. 2017).
20142 LUL Maroon.
20227 White, red & blue with London Underground roundels.

Class 20/0. Standard Design.

20016	B	HN	HNRS	LM (S)
20081	B	HN	HNRS	LM (S)
20088	0	HN	HNRS	LM (S)
20096	B	HN	GBEE	BH
20107	B	HN	GBEE	BH
20118	F0	HN	GBEE	BH	Saltburn-by-the-Sea
20132	F0	HN	GBEE	BH	Barrow Hill Depot
20142	0	20	MOLO	SK	SIR JOHN BETJEMAN
20189	B	20	MOLO	SK	
20205	B	2L	MOLO	SK	
20227	0	2L	MOLO	SK	

Class 20/3. Direct Rail Services refurbished locos. Details as Class 20/0 except:

Refurbished: 15 locomotives were refurbished 1995–96 by Brush Traction at Loughborough (20301–305) or 1997–98 by RFS(E) at Doncaster (20306–315). Disc indicators or headcode panels removed.
Train Brakes: Air.   **Maximum Speed:** 60 mph (+ 75 mph).
Weight: 73 t (+ 76 t).   **Fuel Capacity:** 2909 (+ 4909) litres.
Brake Force: 35 t (+ 31 t).   **RA:** 5 (+ 6).

20301	(20047) r	**DS**	DR	XHSS	BH (S)
20302	(20084) r	**DS**	DR	XHNC	KM
20303	(20127) r	**DS**	DR	XHNC	KM	Max Joule 1958–1999
20304	(20120) r	**DS**	DR	XHSS	BH (S)
20305	(20095) r	**DS**	DR	XHNC	KM	Gresty Bridge
20308	(20187) r+	**DS**	DR	XHNC	KM
20309	(20075) r+	**DS**	DR	XHSS	BH (S)

20311	(20102) r+	**HN** HN	GBEE	BH	
20312	(20042) r+	**DS** DR	XHNC	KM	
20314	(20117) r+	**HN** HN	GBEE	BH	

Class 20/9. Harry Needle Railroad Company (former Hunslet-Barclay/DRS) locos. Details as Class 20/0 except:

Refurbished: 1989 by Hunslet-Barclay at Kilmarnock.
Train Brakes: Air. **Fuel Capacity:** 1727 (+ 4727) litres.
RA: 5 (+ 6).

20901	(20101)		**GB** HN	GBEE	BH
20903	(20083) +		**DR** HN	HNRS	BU (S)
20904	(20041)		**DR** HN	HNRS	BU (S)
20905	(20225) +		**GB** HN	GBEE	BH

CLASS 25   BR/BEYER PEACOCK/SULZER   Bo-Bo

Built: 1965 by Beyer Peacock at Gorton.
Engine: Sulzer 6LDA28-B of 930 kW (1250 hp) at 750 rpm.
Main Generator: AEI RTB15656. **Traction Motors:** AEI 253AY.
Maximum Tractive Effort: 200 kN (45000 lbf).
Continuous Tractive Effort: 93 kN (20800 lbf) at 17.1 mph.
Power at Rail: 708 kW (949 hp). **Train Brakes:** Air & vacuum.
Brake Force: 38 t. **Dimensions:** 15.39 × 2.73 m.
Weight: 71.5 t. **Wheel Diameter:** 1143 mm.
Design Speed: 90 mph. **Maximum Speed:** 60 mph.
Fuel Capacity: 2270 litres. **Route Availability:** 5.
Train Supply: Not equipped.

Carries original number D7628.

Only certified for use on Network Rail tracks between Whitby and Battersby, as an extension of North Yorkshire Moors Railway services.

25278		**GG** NY	MBDL	NY	SYBILLA

CLASS 31   BRUSH/ENGLISH ELECTRIC   A1A-A1A

Built: 1958–62 by Brush Traction at Loughborough.
Engine: English Electric 12SVT of 1100 kW (1470 hp) at 850 rpm.
Main Generator: Brush TG160-48. **Traction Motors:** Brush TM73-68.
Maximum Tractive Effort: 160 kN (35900 lbf).
Continuous Tractive Effort: 83 kN (18700 lbf) at 23.5 mph.
Power at Rail: 872 kW (1170 hp). **Train Brakes:** Air & vacuum.
Brake Force: 49 t. **Dimensions:** 17.30 × 2.67 m.
Weight: 106.7–111 t. **Wheel Diameter:** 1092/1003 mm.
Design Speed: 90 mph. **Maximum Speed:** 90 mph.
Fuel Capacity: 2409 litres. **Route Availability:** 5 or 6.
Train Supply: Not equipped.

Non-standard liveries/numbering:

31190 Also carries the number D5613.
31452 DCR green.

Class 31/1. Standard Design. RA: 5.

31105	**Y**	NR	QADD	ZA	
31106 a	**B**	HJ	RVLO	ZA (S)	
31128	**B**	NS	NRLO	BU	CHARYBDIS
31190	**G**	BA	HTLX	WH	
31233 a	**Y**	NR	QADD	ZA	
31285	**Y**	HN	HNRL	BU (S)	

Class 31/4. Electric Train Supply equipment. RA: 6.
Train Supply: Electric, index 66.

31452	**0**	BA	HTLX	ZA	
31454	**IC**	BA	HTLX	WH (S)	
31459	**K**	HN	RVLO	ZA (S)	CERBERUS
31465	**Y**	HN	HNRL	ZA (S)	
31468	**FR**	BA	RVLO	WO (S)	HYDRA

Class 31/6. ETS through wiring and controls. RA: 5.

31601 (31186)	**DC**	BA	HTLX	WH	Devon Diesel Society
31602 (31191)	**Y**	BA	HTLX	WO (S)	

CLASS 33　　　BRCW/SULZER　　　Bo-Bo

Built: 1960–62 by the Birmingham Railway Carriage & Wagon Company at Smethwick.
Engine: Sulzer 8LDA28 of 1160 kW (1550 hp) at 750 rpm.
Main Generator: Crompton Parkinson CG391B1.
Traction Motors: Crompton Parkinson C171C2.
Maximum Tractive Effort: 200 kN (45000 lbf).
Continuous Tractive Effort: 116 kN (26000 lbf) at 17.5 mph.
Power at Rail: 906 kW (1215 hp). **Train Brakes:** Air & vacuum.
Brake Force: 35 t. **Dimensions:** 15.47 x 2.82 (2.64 m 33/2).
Weight: 76-78 t. **Wheel Diameter:** 1092 mm.
Design Speed: 85 mph. **Maximum Speed:** 85 mph.
Fuel Capacity: 3410 litres. **Route Availability:** 6.
Train Supply: Electric, index 48 (750 V DC only).

Non-standard numbering: 33012 Carries the number D6515.

Class 33/0. Standard Design.

33012	**G**	71	MBDL	Swanage Rly	Lt Jenny Lewis RN
33025	**WC**	WC	AWCX	CS (S)	Glen Falloch
33029	**WC**	WC	AWCX	CS (S)	
33030	**DR**	WC	AWCX	CS (S)	

Class 33/2. Built to former Loading Gauge of Tonbridge–Battle Line.
Equipped with slow speed control.

33207	**WC**	WC	AWCA	CS	Jim Martin

CLASS 37   ENGLISH ELECTRIC   Co-Co

Built: 1960–66 by English Electric at Vulcan Foundry, Newton-le-Willows or by Robert Stephenson & Hawthorns at Darlington.
Engine: English Electric 12CSVT of 1300 kW (1750 hp) at 850 rpm.
Main Generator: English Electric 822/10G.
Traction Motors: English Electric 538/A.
Maximum Tractive Effort: 247 kN (55500 lbf).
Continuous Tractive Effort: 156 kN (35000 lbf) at 13.6 mph.
Power at Rail: 932 kW (1250 hp).   **Train Brakes:** Air & vacuum.
Brake Force: 50 t.   **Dimensions:** 18.75 × 2.74 m.
Weight: 102.8–108.4 t.   **Wheel Diameter:** 1092 mm.
Design Speed: 90 mph.   **Maximum Speed:** 80 mph.
Fuel Capacity: 4046 (+ 7683) litres.   **Route Availability:** 5 (§ 6).
Train Supply: Not equipped.

Non-standard numbering:

37057 Also carries original number D6757.
37424 Also carries the number 37558.
37905 Also carries original number D6838.

Class 37/0. Standard Design.

37025		**BL**	37	COTS	WH	Inverness TMD
37038 a		**DI**	DR	XHNC	KM	
37057		**G**	CS	COTS	WH	
37059 ar+	**DI**	DR	XHNC	KM	
37069 ar+	**DI**	DR	XHNC	KM	
37099		**B**	CS	COLS	BH (S)	
37116 +	**CS**	CS	COTS	WH	
37146		**CE**	CS	COLS	Leeming Bar (S)	
37165 a+	**CE**	WC	AWCX	CS (S)	
37175 a	**CS**	CS	COTS	WH	
37188		**F**	CS	COLS	BH (S)	
37194 a+	**DS**	DR	XHSS	ZA (S)	
37198 +	**Y**	NR	MBDL	BU (S)	CHIEF ENGINEER
37207		**B**	CS	COLS	BH (S)	
37214		**WC**	WC	AWCX	CS (S)	
37218 ar+	**DI**	DR	XHNC	KM	
37219		**CS**	CS	COTS	WH	
37254		**IC**	CS	COTS	WH	
37259 ar	**DS**	DR	XHNC	KM	

Class 37/4. Refurbished with electric train supply equipment. Main generator replaced by alternator. Regeared (CP7) bogies. Details as Class 37/0 except:
Main Alternator: Brush BA1005A.   **Power At Rail:** 935 kW (1254 hp).
Traction Motors: English Electric 538/5A.
Maximum Tractive Effort: 256 kN (57440 lbf).
Continuous Tractive Effort: 184 kN (41250 lbf) at 11.4 mph.
Weight: 107 t.   **Design Speed:** 80 mph.
Fuel Capacity: 7683 litres.
Train Supply: Electric, index 30.

37401 ar	**BL**	DR	XHCC	KM	Mary Queen of Scots
37402 a	**BL**	DR	XHCC	KM	Stephen Middlemore 23.12.1954–8.6.2013
37403	**BL**	SP	XHAC	KM	Isle of Mull
37405 ar	**DS**	DR	XHAC	KM	
37407	**F**	DR	XHAC	KM	
37409 ar	**DS**	DR	XHCC	KM	Lord Hinton
37413	**E**	DR	XHSS	ZA (S)	
37419 ar	**DS**	DR	XHAC	KM	Carl Haviland 1954–2012
37421	**CS**	CS	COTS	WH	
37422 ar	**DR**	DR	XHAC	KM	
37423 ar	**DI**	DR	XHCC	KM	Spirit of the Lakes
37424	**BL**	DR	XHAC	KM	Avro Vulcan XH558
37425 ar	**DS**	DR	XHAC	KM	Sir Robert McAlpine/Concrete Bob

Class 37/5. Refurbished without train supply equipment. Main generator replaced by alternator. Regeared (CP7) bogies. Details as Class 37/4 except:
Power At Rail: 932 kW (1250 hp).
Maximum Tractive Effort: 248 kN (55590 lbf).
Continuous Tractive Effort: 184 kN (41250 lbf) at 11.4 mph.
Weight: 106.1–110.0 t.

37503 r§	**E**	EP	EPUK	LR (S)	
37510 a	**DS**	EP	EPUK	LR (S)	
37516 s	**WC**	WC	AWCA	CS	Loch Laidon
37517 as	**LH**	WC	AWCX	CS (S)	
37518 ar	**WC**	WC	AWCA	CS	

Class 37/6. Originally refurbished for Nightstar services. Main generator replaced by alternator. UIC jumpers. Details as Class 37/5 except:
Maximum Speed: 90 mph. **Train Brake**: Air.
Train Supply: Not equipped, but electric through wired.

37601 a	**DS**	DR	XHNC	KM	Class 37-'Fifty'
37602 ar	**DS**	DR	XHNC	KM	
37603 a	**DS**	DR	XHNC	KM	
37604 a	**DS**	DR	XHNC	KM	
37605 ar	**DS**	DR	XHNC	KM	
37606 a	**DS**	DR	XHNC	KM	
37607 a	**DS**	DR	XHNC	KM	
37608 ar	**DR**	EP	EPUK	LR	
37609 a	**DI**	DR	XHNC	KM	
37610 ar	**DS**	DR	XHNC	KM	T.S.(Ted) Cassady 14.5.61–6.4.08
37611 a	**DR**	EP	EPUK	LR	
37612 a	**DS**	DR	XHNC	KM	

Class 37/5 continued.

37667 ars	**DS**	DR	XHNC	KM	
37668 e	**WC**	WC	AWCA	CS	
37669 e	**WC**	WC	AWCA	CS	
37670 r	**DB**	EP	EPUK	BH (S)	
37676 a	**WC**	WC	AWCA	CS (S)	Loch Rannoch
37682 ar	**DS**	DR	XHSS	ZA (S)	
37685 a	**WC**	WC	AWCA	CS	Loch Arkaig

37688	ar	**DS** DR	XHNC	KM	Kingmoor TMD

Class 37/7. Refurbished locos. Main generator replaced by alternator. Regeared (CP7) bogies. Ballast weights added. Details as Class 37/5 except:
Main Alternator: GEC G564AZ (37796–803). Brush BA1005A (others).
Maximum Tractive Effort: 276 kN (62000 lbf).
Weight: 120 t. **Route Availability:** 7.

37703		**DR** DR	XHHP	BO
37706		**WC** WC	AWCA	CS
37710		**LH** WC	AWCX	CS (S)
37712	a	**WC** WC	AWCX	CS (S)
37716		**DI** DR	XHNC	KM
37800	d	**EX** EP	GROG	LR
37884	d	**EX** EP	GROG	LR

Class 37/9. Refurbished locos. New power unit. Main generator replaced by alternator. Ballast weights added. Details as Class 37/4 except:
Engine: * Mirrlees 6MB275T of 1340 kW (1800 hp) or † Ruston 6RK270T of 1340 kW (1800 hp) at 900 rpm.
Main Alternator: Brush BA15005A.
Train supply: Not equipped.
Maximum Tractive Effort: 279 kN (62680 lbf).
Weight: 120 t. **Route Availability:** 7.

37901	*	**FO** CS	COLS	SE (S)
37905	†	**G** UR	UKRM	LR
37906	†	**FO** UR	UKRM	LR (S)

Class 97/3. Class 37s refurbished for Network Rail for use on the Cambrian Lines which are signalled by ERTMS. Details as Class 37/0.

97301	(37100) e	**Y**	NR	QETS	ZA
97302	(37170) e	**Y**	NR	QETS	ZA
97303	(37178) e	**Y**	NR	QETS	ZA
97304	(37217) e	**Y**	NR	QETS	ZA	John Tiley

CLASS 40   ENGLISH ELECTRIC   1Co-Co1

Built: 1961 by English Electric at Vulcan Foundry, Newton-le-Willows.
Engine: English Electric 16SVT Mk2 of 1492 kW (2000 hp) at 850 rpm.
Main Generator: English Electric 822/4C.
Traction Motors: English Electric 526/5D or EE526/7D.
Maximum Tractive Effort: 231 kN (52000 lbf).
Continuous Tractive Effort: 137 kN (30900 lbf) at 18.8 mph.
Power at Rail: 1160 kW (1550 hp). **Train Brakes:** Air & vacuum.
Brake Force: 51 t. **Dimensions:** 21.18 x ? 78 m.
Weight: 132 t. **Wheel Diameter:** 914/1143 mm.
Design Speed: 90 mph. **Maximum Speed:** 90 mph.
Fuel Capacity: 3250 litres. **Route Availability:** 6.
Train Supply: Steam heating.

Currently carries original number 345.

40145		**B** 40	ELRD	BQ

CLASS 43   BREL/PAXMAN   Bo-Bo

Built: 1975–82 by BREL at Crewe Works.
Engine: MTU 16V4000R41R of 1680kW (2250 hp) at 1500 rpm.
(* Paxman 12VP185 of 1565 kW (2100 hp) at 1500 rpm.)
Main Alternator: Brush BA1001B.
Traction Motors: Brush TMH68–46 or GEC G417AZ (43124–152); frame mounted.
Maximum Tractive Effort: 80 kN (17980 lbf).
Continuous Tractive Effort: 46 kN (10340 lbf) at 64.5 mph.
Power at Rail: 1320 kW (1770 hp).   **Train Brakes:** Air.
Brake Force: 35 t.   **Dimensions:** 17.79 x 2.74 m.
Weight: 70.25–75.0 t.   **Wheel Diameter:** 1020 mm.
Design Speed: 125 mph.   **Maximum Speed:** 125 mph.
Fuel Capacity: 4500 litres.   **Route Availability:** 5.
Train Supply: Three-phase electric.

† Buffer fitted.

43013, 43014 & 43062 are fitted with measuring apparatus & front-end cameras.

Power cars 43013, 43321 and 43423 carry small commemorative plates to celebrate 40 years of the HST, reading "40 YEARS 1976–2016".

Non-standard and Advertising liveries:

43002 – Original HST BR blue & yellow.
43027 – 90 Glorious Years (blue).
43126 & 43148 Bristol 2015 – European Green Capital (green & white).
43144 & 43146 – Building a Greater West.
43163 – Visit Plymouth (blue).
43172 – We Shall Remember Them (various).
43238 – National Railway Museum 40 Years.

43002	**O**	A	EFPC	LA	Sir Kenneth Grange
43003	**FB**	A	EFPC	LA	ISAMBARD KINGDOM BRUNEL
43004	**FB**	A	EFPC	LA	First for the future/
					First ar gyfer y dyfodol
43005	**GW**	A	EFPC	LA	
43009	**FB**	A	EFPC	LA	
43010	**FB**	A	EFPC	LA	
43012	**FB**	A	EFPC	LA	Exeter Panel Signal Box
					21st Anniversary 2009
43013 †	**Y**	P	QCAR	EC	
43014 †	**Y**	P	QCAR	EC	The Railway Observer
43015	**FB**	A	EFPC	LA	
43016	**FB**	A	EFPC	LA	
43017	**FB**	A	EFPC	LA	Hannahs discoverhannahs.org
43018	**FB**	A	EFPC	LA	
43020	**FB**	A	EFPC	LA	MTU Power. Passion. Partnership
43021	**FB**	A	EFPC	LA	David Austin – Cartoonist
43022	**FB**	A	EFPC	LA	The Duke of Edinburgh's Award
					Diamond Anniversary 1956–2016
43023	**FB**	A	EFPC	LA	SQN LDR HAROLD STARR
					ONE OF THE FEW

43024	**FB**	A	EFPC	LA	Great Western Society 1961–2011 Didcot Railway Centre
43025	**FB**	A	EFPC	LA	IRO The Institution of Railway Operators 2000–2010 TEN YEARS PROMOTING OPERATIONAL EXCELLENCE
43026	**FB**	A	EFPC	LA	Michael Eavis
43027	**AL**	A	EFPC	LA	
43028	**FB**	A	EFPC	LA	
43029	**FB**	A	EFPC	LA	
43030	**FB**	A	EFPC	LA	Christian Lewis Trust
43031	**FB**	A	EFPC	LA	
43032	**FB**	A	EFPC	LA	
43033	**FB**	A	EFPC	LA	Driver Brian Cooper 15 June 1947–5 October 1999
43034	**FB**	A	EFPC	LA	TravelWatch SouthWest
43035	**FB**	A	EFPC	LA	
43036	**FB**	A	EFPC	LA	
43037	**FB**	A	EFPC	LA	PENYDARREN
43040	**FB**	A	EFPC	LA	Bristol St. Philip's Marsh
43041	**GW**	A	EFPC	LE	Meningitis Trust Support for Life
43042	**FB**	A	EFPC	LE	
43043 *	**ST**	P	EMPC	NL	
43044 *	**ST**	P	EMPC	NL	
43045 *	**ST**	P	EMPC	NL	
43046 *	**ST**	P	EMPC	NL	
43047 *	**ST**	P	EMPC	NL	
43048 *	**ST**	P	EMPC	NL	T.C.B. Miller MBE
43049 *	**ST**	P	EMPC	NL	Neville Hill
43050 *	**ST**	P	EMPC	NL	
43052 *	**ST**	P	EMPC	NL	
43053	**FB**	P	EFPC	LE	University of Worcester
43054 *	**ST**	P	EMPC	NL	
43055 *	**ST**	P	EMPC	NL	The Sheffield Star 125 Years
43056	**FB**	P	EFPC	LE	The Royal British Legion
43058 *	**ST**	P	EMPC	NL	
43059 *	**ST**	P	EMPC	NL	
43060 *	**ST**	P	EMPC	NL	
43061 *	**ST**	P	EMPC	NL	
43062	**Y**	P	QCAR	EC	John Armitt
43063	**FB**	P	EFPC	LE	
43064 *	**ST**	P	EMPC	NL	
43066 *	**ST**	P	EMPC	NL	
43069	**FB**	P	EFPC	LE	
43070	**FB**	P	EFPC	LE	The Corps of Royal Electrical and Mechanical Engineers
43071	**FR**	P	EFPC	LE	
43073 *	**ST**	P	EMPC	NL	
43075 *	**ST**	P	EMPC	NL	
43076 *	**ST**	P	EMPC	NL	IN SUPPORT OF HELP for HEROES
43078	**FB**	P	EFPC	LE	
43079	**FB**	P	EFPC	LE	

43081 *	**ST**	P	EMPC	NL	
43082 *	**ST**	P	EMPC	NL	RAILWAY children – THE VOICE FOR STREET CHILDREN WORLDWIDE
43083 *	**ST**	P	EMPC	NL	
43086	**FB**	P	EFPC	LE	
43087	**FB**	P	EFPC	LE	11 Explosive Ordnance Disposal Regiment Royal Logistic Corps
43088	**FB**	P	EFPC	LE	
43089 *	**ST**	P	EMPC	NL	
43091	**FB**	P	EFPC	LE	
43092	**FB**	FG	EFPC	LE	
43093	**FB**	FG	EFPC	LE	
43094	**FB**	FG	EFPC	LE	
43097	**FB**	FG	EFPC	LE	Environment Agency
43098	**FB**	FG	EFPC	LE	
43122	**FB**	FG	EFPC	LE	
43124	**FB**	A	EFPC	LE	
43125	**FB**	A	EFPC	LE	
43126	**AL**	A	EFPC	LE	
43127	**FB**	A	EFPC	LE	Sir Peter Parker 1924–2002 Cotswold Line 150
43128	**FB**	A	EFPC	LE	
43129	**FB**	A	EFPC	LE	
43130	**FB**	A	EFPC	LE	
43131	**FB**	A	EFPC	LE	
43132	**FB**	A	EFPC	LE	We Save the Children – Will You?
43133	**FB**	A	EFPC	LE	
43134	**FB**	A	EFPC	LE	
43135	**FB**	A	EFPC	LE	
43136	**FB**	A	EFPC	LE	
43137	**FB**	A	EFPC	LE	Newton Abbot 150
43138	**FB**	A	EFPC	LE	
43139	**FB**	A	EFPC	LE	Driver Stan Martin 25 June 1950 – 6 November 2004
43140	**FB**	A	EFPC	LE	Landore Diesel Depot 1963 Celebrating 50 years 2013/ Depo Diesel Glandŵr 1963 Dathlu 50 Mlynedd 2013
43141	**FB**	A	EFPC	LE	Cardiff Panel Signal Box 1966–2016/ Blwch Signalau Panel Caerdydd 1966–2016
43142	**FB**	A	EFPC	LE	Reading Panel Signal Box 1965–2010
43143	**FB**	A	EFPC	LE	Stroud 700
43144	**AL**	A	EFPC	LE	
43145	**FB**	A	EFPC	LE	
43146	**AL**	A	EFPC	LE	
43147	**FB**	A	EFPC	LE	Royal Marines Celebrating 350 Years
43148	**AL**	A	EFPC	LE	
43149	**FB**	A	EFPC	LE	University of Plymouth
43150	**FB**	A	EFPC	LE	

43151	**FB**	A	EFPC	LE	
43152	**FB**	A	EFPC	LE	
43153	**FB**	FG	EFPC	OO	
43154	**FB**	FG	EFPC	OO	
43155	**FB**	FG	EFPC	OO	The Red Arrows 50 Seasons of Excellence
43156	**FB**	P	EFPC	OO	Dartington International Summer School
43158	**FB**	FG	EFPC	OO	
43159	**FB**	P	EFPC	OO	
43160	**FB**	P	EFPC	OO	Sir Moir Lockhead OBE
43161	**FB**	P	EFPC	OO	
43162	**FB**	P	EFPC	OO	
43163	**AL**	A	EFPC	OO	
43164	**FB**	A	EFPC	OO	
43165	**FB**	A	EFPC	OO	Prince Michael of Kent
43168	**FB**	A	EFPC	OO	
43169	**FB**	A	EFPC	OO	THE NATIONAL TRUST
43170	**FB**	A	EFPC	OO	
43171	**FB**	A	EFPC	OO	
43172	**AL**	A	EFPC	OO	Harry Patch – The last survivor of the trenches
43174	**FB**	A	EFPC	OO	
43175	**FB**	A	EFPC	OO	GWR 175TH ANNIVERSARY
43176	**FB**	A	EFPC	OO	
43177	**FB**	A	EFPC	OO	
43179	**FB**	A	EFPC	OO	Pride of Laira
43180	**FB**	P	EFPC	OO	
43181	**FB**	A	EFPC	OO	
43182	**FB**	A	EFPC	OO	
43183	**FB**	A	EFPC	OO	
43185	**IC**	A	EFPC	OO	Great Western
43186	**FB**	A	EFPC	OO	
43187	**GW**	A	EFPC	OO	
43188	**GW**	A	EFPC	OO	
43189	**FB**	A	EFPC	OO	RAILWAY HERITAGE TRUST
43190	**FB**	A	EFPC	OO	
43191	**FB**	A	EFPC	OO	
43192	**FB**	A	EFPC	OO	
43193	**FB**	P	EFPC	OO	
43194	**FB**	FG	EFPC	OO	
43195	**FB**	P	EFPC	OO	
43196	**FB**	P	EFPC	OO	
43197	**FB**	P	EFPC	OO	
43198	**FB**	FG	EFPC	OO	Oxfordshire 2007

Class 43/2. Rebuilt Virgin Trains East Coast, CrossCountry and Grand Central power cars. Power cars have been renumbered by adding 200 to their original number or 400 to their original number (Grand Central), except 43123 which became 43423.

43206	(43006)	**VE**	A	IECP	EC
43207	(43007)	**XC**	A	EHPC	EC

43208 (43008)	**VE**	A	IECP	EC	Lincolnshire Echo
43238 (43038)	**AL**	A	IECP	EC	National Railway Museum 40 Years 1975–2015
43239 (43039)	**VE**	A	IECP	EC	
43251 (43051)	**VE**	P	IECP	EC	
43257 (43057)	**VE**	P	IECP	EC	
43272 (43072)	**VE**	P	IECP	EC	
43274 (43074)	**VE**	P	IECP	EC	Spirit of Sunderland
43277 (43077)	**VE**	P	IECP	EC	
43285 (43085)	**XC**	P	EHPC	EC	
43290 (43090)	**VE**	P	IECP	EC	mtu fascination of power
43295 (43095)	**VE**	A	IECP	EC	
43296 (43096)	**VE**	A	IECP	EC	
43299 (43099)	**VE**	P	IECP	EC	
43300 (43100)	**VE**	P	IECP	EC	Craigentinny 100 YEARS 1914–2014
43301 (43101)	**XC**	P	EHPC	EC	
43302 (43102)	**VE**	P	IECP	EC	
43303 (43103)	**XC**	P	EHPC	EC	
43304 (43104)	**XC**	A	EHPC	EC	
43305 (43105)	**VE**	A	IECP	EC	
43306 (43106)	**VE**	A	IECP	EC	
43307 (43107)	**VE**	A	IECP	EC	
43308 (43108)	**VE**	A	IECP	EC	HIGHLAND CHIEFTAIN
43309 (43109)	**VE**	A	IECP	EC	
43310 (43110)	**VE**	A	IECP	EC	
43311 (43111)	**VE**	A	IECP	EC	
43312 (43112)	**VE**	A	IECP	EC	
43313 (43113)	**VE**	A	IECP	EC	
43314 (43114)	**VE**	A	IECP	EC	
43315 (43115)	**VE**	A	IECP	EC	
43316 (43116)	**VE**	A	IECP	EC	
43317 (43117)	**VE**	A	IECP	EC	
43318 (43118)	**VE**	A	IECP	EC	
43319 (43119)	**VE**	A	IECP	EC	
43320 (43120)	**VE**	A	IECP	EC	
43321 (43121)	**XC**	P	EHPC	EC	
43357 (43157)	**XC**	P	EHPC	EC	
43366 (43166)	**XC**	A	EHPC	EC	
43367 (43167)	**VE**	A	IECP	EC	DELTIC 50 1955–2005
43378 (43178)	**XC**	A	EHPC	EC	
43384 (43184)	**XC**	A	EHPC	EC	
43423 (43123) †	**GC**	A	GCHP	HT	'VALENTA' 1972–2010
43465 (43065) †	**GC**	A	GCHP	HT	
43467 (43067) †	**GC**	A	GCHP	HT	
43468 (43068) †	**GC**	A	GCHP	HT	
43480 (43080) †	**GC**	A	GCHP	HT	
43484 (43084) †	**GC**	A	GCHP	HT	PETER FOX 1942–2011 PLATFORM 5

CLASS 47   BR/BRUSH/SULZER   Co-Co

Built: 1963–67 by Brush Traction, at Loughborough or by BR at Crewe Works.
Engine: Sulzer 12LDA28C of 1920 kW (2580 hp) at 750 rpm.
Main Generator: Brush TG160-60 Mk4 or TM172-50 Mk1.
Traction Motors: Brush TM64-68 Mk1 or Mk1A.
Maximum Tractive Effort: 267 kN (60000 lbf).
Continuous Tractive Effort: 133 kN (30000 lbf) at 26 mph.
Power at Rail: 1550 kW (2080 hp).   **Train Brakes:** Air.
Brake Force: 61 t.   **Dimensions:** 19.38 x 2.79 m.
Weight: 111.5–120.6 t.   **Wheel Diameter:** 1143 mm.
Design Speed: 95 mph.
Maximum Speed: 95 mph.
Fuel Capacity: 3273 (+ 5887).   **Route Availability:** 6 or 7.
Train Supply: Not equipped.

Class 47s exported for use abroad are listed in section 6 of this book.

Non-standard liveries/numbering:

47270	Also carries original number 1971.
47501	Also carried original number D1944.
47773	Also carries original number D1755.
47798	Royal Train claret with Rail Express Systems markings.
47830	Also carries original number D1645.

Class 47/0 (Dual-braked locos). Standard Design. Details as above.

47194	a+	**F**	WC AWCX	CS (S)	
47236	+	**FE**	WC AWCX	CS (S)	
47237	+	**WC**	WC AWCA	CS	
47245	+	**WC**	WC AWCA	CS	
47270	a+	**B**	WC AWCA	CS	SWIFT

Class 47/3 (Dual-braked locos).
Details as Class 47/0 except: **Weight:** 113.7 t.

47355	a+	**K**	WC AWCX	CS (S)
47368	+	**F**	WC AWCX	CS (S)

Class 47/4. Electric Train Supply equipment.
Details as Class 47/0 except:

Weight: 120.4–125.1 t.   **Fuel Capacity:** 3273 (+ 5537) litres.
Train Supply: Electric, index 66.   **Route Availability:** 7.

47492	x	**RX**	WC AWCX	CS (S)	
47500	x	**WC**	WC AWCX	CS (S)	
47501	x+	**GG**	LS MBDL	CI	CRAFTSMAN
47526	x	**BI**	WC AWCX	CS (S)	
47580	x	**BL**	47 MBDL	TM	County of Essex

Class 47/7. Former Railnet dedicated locos. Details as Class 47/0 except:
Fuel Capacity: 5887 litres.

47727	**CS**	CS COLS	WH (S)	Rebecca

47739	**CS**	CS	COFS	WH	Robin of Templecombe 1938-2013
47746 x	**WC**	WC	AWCA	CS	Chris Fudge 29.7.70 – 22.6.10
47749	**CS**	CS	COFS	WH	CITY OF TRURO
47760 x	**WC**	WC	AWCA	CS	
47768	**RX**	WC	AWCX	CS (S)	
47769	**V**	HN	HNRS	BH (S)	Resolve
47772 x	**RX**	WC	AWCX	CS (S)	
47773 x	**GG**	70	MBDL	TM	
47776 x	**RX**	WC	AWCX	CS (S)	
47786	**WC**	WC	AWCA	CS	Roy Castle OBE
47787	**WC**	WC	AWCX	CS (S)	Windsor Castle
47790	**VN**	LS	MBDL	CL	

Class 47/4 continued. RA6.

47798 x	**O**	NM	MBDL	YK	Prince William
47802 +	**WC**	WC	AWCA	CS	
47804	**WC**	WC	AWCA	CS	
47805 +	**DS**	LS	MBDL	CL	
47810 +	**DI**	AF	MBDL	ZG	
47811 +	**GL**	FL	DHLT	BA (S)	
47812 +	**RB**	RO	GROG	BU	
47813 +	**DS**	DR	XHSS	KM (S)	Solent
47815 +	**RB**	RO	GROG	BU	
47816 +	**GL**	FL	DHLT	BA (S)	
47818 +	**DS**	AF	MBDL	ZG	
47826 +	**WC**	WC	AWCA	CS	
47830 +	**GG**	FL	DFLH	LD	BEECHING'S LEGACY
47832 +	**WC**	WC	AWCA	CS	
47841 +	**DS**	LS	MBDL	ZG (S)	
47843 +	**RB**	RO	GROG	BU	
47847 +	**BL**	RO	GROG	BU	
47848 +	**RB**	RO	GROG	BU	
47851 +	**WC**	WC	AWCA	CS	
47853 +	**DR**	HN	GBHN	BH (S)	
47854 +	**WC**	WC	AWCA	CS	Diamond Jubilee

CLASS 50   ENGLISH ELECTRIC   Co-Co

Built: 1967–68 by English Electric at Vulcan Foundry, Newton-le-Willows.
Engine: English Electric 16CVST of 2010 kW (2700 hp) at 850 rpm.
Main Generator: English Electric 840/4B.
Traction Motors: English Electric 538/5A.
Maximum Tractive Effort: 216 kN (48500 lbf).
Continuous Tractive Effort: 147 kN (33000 lbf) at 23.5 mph.
Power at Rail: 1540 kW (2070 hp).   **Train Brakes:** Air & vacuum.
Brake Force: 59 t.   **Dimensions:** 20.88 x 2.78 m.
Weight: 116.9 t.   **Wheel Diameter:** 1092 mm.
Design Speed: 105 mph.   **Maximum Speed:** 90 mph.
Fuel Capacity: 4796 litres.   **Route Availability:** 6.
Train Supply: Electric, index 61.

Non-standard numbering:

50050   Also carries original number D400.

50007	B	NB	MBDL	WH	Hercules
50017	N	NB	MBDL	WH	Royal Oak
50044	B	50	CFOL	KR	Exeter
50049	BL	50	CFOL	KR	Defiance
50050	B	NB	MBDL	WH	Fearless

CLASS 52   BR/MAYBACH   C-C

Built: 1961–64 by BR at Swindon Works.
Engine: Two Maybach MD655 of 1007 kW (1350 hp) each at 1500 rpm.
Transmission: Hydraulic. Voith L630rV.
Maximum Tractive Effort: 297 kN (66700 lbf).
Continuous Tractive Effort: 201 kN (45200 lbf) at 14.5 mph.
Power at Rail: 1490 kW (2000 hp).   **Train Brakes:** Air & vacuum.
Brake Force: 83 t.   **Dimensions:** 20.70 m x 2.78 m.
Weight: 110 t.   **Wheel Diameter:** 1092 mm.
Design Speed: 90 mph.   **Maximum Speed:** 90 mph.
Fuel Capacity: 3900 litres.   **Route Availability:** 6.
Train Supply: Steam heating.

Never allocated a number in the 1972 number series.

D1015	M	DT	MBDL	TM	WESTERN CHAMPION

CLASS 55   ENGLISH ELECTRIC   Co-Co

Built: 1961 by English Electric at Vulcan Foundry, Newton-le-Willows.
Engine: Two Napier-Deltic D18-25 of 1230 kW (1650 hp) each at 1500 rpm.
Main Generators: Two English Electric 829/1A.
Traction Motors: English Electric 538/A.
Maximum Tractive Effort: 222 kN (50000 lbf).
Continuous Tractive Effort: 136 kN (30500 lbf) at 32.5 mph.
Power at Rail: 1969 kW (2640 hp).   **Train Brakes:** Air & vacuum.
Brake Force: 51 t.   **Dimensions:** 21.18 x 2.68 m.
Weight: 100 t.   **Wheel Diameter:** 1092 mm.
Design Speed: 105 mph.   **Maximum Speed:** 100 mph.
Fuel Capacity: 3755 litres.   **Route Availability:** 5.
Train Supply: Electric, index 66.

55002	GG	NM	MBDL	YK	THE KING'S OWN YORKSHIRE LIGHT INFANTRY
55009	B	DP	MBDL	BH	ALYCIDON
55022	B	MW	MBDL	NY	ROYAL SCOTS GREY

56007–56128
41

CLASS 56 BRUSH/BR/RUSTON Co-Co

Built: 1976–84 by Electroputere at Craiova, Romania (as sub-contractors for Brush) or BREL at Doncaster or Crewe Works.
Engine: Ruston Paxman 16RK3CT of 2460 kW (3250 hp) at 900 rpm.
Main Alternator: Brush BA1101A.
Traction Motors: Brush TM73-62.
Maximum Tractive Effort: 275 kN (61800 lbf).
Continuous Tractive Effort: 240 kN (53950 lbf) at 16.8 mph.
Power at Rail: 1790 kW (2400 hp). **Train Brakes:** Air.
Brake Force: 60 t. **Dimensions:** 19.36 x 2.79 m.
Weight: 126 t. **Wheel Diameter:** 1143 mm.
Design Speed: 80 mph. **Maximum Speed:** 80 mph.
Fuel Capacity: 5228 litres. **Route Availability:** 7.
Train Supply: Not equipped.

All equipped with Slow Speed Control.

Class 56s exported for use abroad are listed in section 6 of this book.

Non-standard liveries:

56009 All over blue.

56303 All over dark green.

56007	**B**	UR	UKRS	LR (S)	
56009	**O**	UR	UKRS	BL (S)	
56018	**FER**	UR	UKRS	LB (S)	
56031	**FER**	UR	UKRS	LR (S)	
56032	**FER**	UR	UKRS	LR (S)	
56037	**E**	UR	UKRS	LR (S)	
56038	**FER**	UR	UKRS	LR (S)	
56049	**CS**	CS	COLS	WH (S)	
56051	**FER**	CS	COLS	WH (S)	
56060	**FER**	UR	UKRS	LB (S)	
56065	**FER**	UR	UKRS	LR (S)	
56069	**FER**	UR	UKRS	LR (S)	
56077	**LH**	UR	UKRS	LR (S)	
56078	**CS**	CS	COFS	WH	
56081	**FO**	UR	UKRL	LR	
56087	**CS**	CS	COFS	WH	
56090	**CS**	CS	COLS	WH (S)	
56091	**FER**	BA	HTLX	WH	
56094	**CS**	CS	COLS	WH (S)	
56096	**CS**	CS	COLS	WH (S)	
56098	**FO**	UR	UKRL	LR	Lost Boys 68–88
56103	**FER**	BA	HTLX	WH	
56104	**FO**	UR	UKRL	LR	
56105	**CS**	CS	COFS	WH	
56106	**FER**	UR	UKRS	LR (S)	
56113	**CS**	CS	COFS	WH	
56128	**F**	BA	HTLX	WH (S)	

56301	(56045)	**FA**	56	UKRL	LR
56302	(56124)	**CS**	CS	COFS	WH
56303	(56125)	**O**	BA	HTLX	WH
56311	(56057)	**DC**	BA	HTLX	WH
56312	(56003)	**DC**	BA	HTLX	WH

56302: PECO The Railway Modeller 2016 40 Years

56312: Jeremiah Dixon Son of County Durham Surveyor of the Mason-Dixon Line U.S.A.

CLASS 57   BRUSH/GM   Co-Co

Built: 1964–65 by Brush Traction at Loughborough or BR at Crewe Works as Class 47. Rebuilt 1997–2004 by Brush Traction at Loughborough.
Engine: General Motors 12 645 E3 of 1860 kW (2500 hp) at 904 rpm.
Main Alternator: Brush BA1101D (recovered from Class 56).
Traction Motors: Brush TM64-68 Mark 1 or Mark 1A.
Maximum Tractive Effort: 244.5 kN (55000 lbf).
Continuous Tractive Effort: 140 kN (31500 lbf) at ?? mph.
Power at Rail: 1507 kW (2025 hp).
Brake Force: 80 t.
Weight: 120.6 t.
Design Speed: 75 mph.
Fuel Capacity: 5550 litres.
Train Supply: Not equipped.
Train Brakes: Air.
Dimensions: 19.38 x 2.79 m.
Wheel Diameter: 1143 mm.
Maximum Speed: 75 mph.
Route Availability: 6

Non-standard livery: 57604 – Original Great Western Railway green.

Class 57/0. No Train Supply Equipment. Rebuilt 1997–2000.

57001	(47356)	**WC**	WC	AWCA	CS
57002	(47322)	**DI**	DR	XHCK	KM
57003	(47317)	**DI**	DR	XHCK	KM
57004	(47347)	**DS**	DR	XHSS	LW (S)
57005	(47350)	**AZ**	WC	AWCX	CS (S)
57006	(47187)	**WC**	WC	AWCX	CS (S)
57007	(47332)	**DI**	DR	XHCK	KM
57008	(47060)	**DS**	DR	XHSS	LW (S)
57009	(47079)	**DS**	DR	XHSS	LW (S)
57010	(47231)	**DI**	DR	XHSS	LW (S)
57011	(47329)	**DS**	DR	XHSS	LW (S)
57012	(47204)	**DS**	DR	XHSS	LW (S)

Class 57/3. Electric Train Supply Equipment. Former Virgin Trains locos. Rebuilt 2002–04. Details as Class 57/0 except:

Engine: General Motors 12645E3B of 2050 kW (2750 hp) at 954 rpm.
Main Alternator: Brush BA1101F (recovered from Class 56) or Brush BA1101G.
Fuel Capacity: 5887 litres.
Design Speed: 95 mph.
Brake Force: 60 t.
Train Supply: Electric, index 100.
Maximum Speed: 95 mph.
Weight: 117 t.

57301–57605　　　　　　　　　　　　　　　　　　　　　　　　　　43

57301 (47845) d	**DI**	P	XHAC	KM	Goliath
57302 (47827) d	**DS**	DR	XHVT	KM	Chad Varah
57303 (47705) d	**DI**	P	XHAC	KM	Pride of Carlisle
57304 (47807) d	**DS**	DR	XHVT	KM	Pride of Cheshire
57305 (47822) d	**VN**	P	XHAC	KM	Northern Princess
57306 (47814) d	**DI**	P	XHAC	KM	Her Majesty's Railway Inspectorate 175
57307 (47225) d	**DR**	DR	XHVT	KM	LADY PENELOPE
57308 (47846) d	**DS**	DR	XHVT	KM	County of Staffordshire
57309 (47806) d	**DI**	DR	XHVT	KM	Pride of Crewe
57310 (47831) d	**DI**	P	XHAC	KM	Pride of Cumbria
57311 (47817) d	**DS**	DR	XHVT	KM	Thunderbird
57312 (47330) d	**VN**	P	XHAC	KM	Solway Princess
57313 (47371)	**WC**	WC	AWCA	CS	
57314 (47372)	**WC**	WC	AWCA	CS	
57315 (47234)	**WC**	WC	AWCA	CS	
57316 (47290)	**WC**	WC	AWCA	CS	

Class 57/6. Electric Train Supply Equipment. Prototype ETS loco. Rebuilt 2001. Details as Class 57/0 except:

Main Alternator: Brush BA1101E.
Train Supply: Electric, index 95.
Design Speed: 95 mph.
Brake Force: 60 t.
Fuel Capacity: 3273 litres.
Weight: 113t.
Maximum Speed: 95 mph.

57601 (47825)　　**WC**　WC　AWCA　　CS

Class 57/6. Electric Train Supply Equipment. Great Western Railway locos. Rebuilt 2004. Details as Class 57/3.

57602 (47337)	**GW**	P	EFOO	OO	Restormel Castle
57603 (47349)	**GW**	P	EFOO	OO	Tintagel Castle
57604 (47209)	**O**	P	EFOO	OO	PENDENNIS CASTLE
57605 (47206)	**GW**	P	EFOO	OO	Totnes Castle

CLASS 59　　　GENERAL MOTORS　　　Co-Co

Built: 1985 (59001–004) or 1989 (59005) by General Motors, La Grange, Illinois, USA or 1990 (59101–104), 1994 (59201) and 1995 (59202–206) by General Motors, London, Ontario, Canada.
Engine: General Motors 16-645E3C two stroke of 2460 kW (3300 hp) at 904 rpm.
Main Alternator: General Motors AR11 MLD-D14A.
Traction Motors: General Motors D77B.
Maximum Tractive Effort: 506 kN (113550 lbf).
Continuous Tractive Effort: 291 kN (65300 lbf) at 14.3 mph.
Power at Rail: 1889 kW (2533 hp).
Brake Force: 69 t.
Weight: 121 t.
Design Speed: 60 (* 75) mph.
Fuel Capacity: 4546 litres.
Train Supply: Not equipped.
Train Brakes: Air.
Dimensions: 21.35 x 2.65 m.
Wheel Diameter: 1067 mm.
Maximum Speed: 60 (* 75) mph.
Route Availability: 7.

Class 59/0. Owned by Aggregate Industries and GB Railfreight.

59001	**AI**	AI	XYPO	MD	YEOMAN ENDEAVOUR
59002	**AI**	AI	XYPO	MD	ALAN J DAY
59003	**GB**	GB	GBYH	PG	YEOMAN HIGHLANDER
59004	**FY**	AI	XYPO	MD	PAUL A HAMMOND
59005	**AI**	AI	XYPO	MD	KENNETH J PAINTER

Class 59/1. Owned by Hanson UK.

59101	**HA**	HA	XYPA	MD	Village of Whatley
59102	**HA**	HA	XYPA	MD	Village of Chantry
59103	**HA**	HA	XYPA	MD	Village of Mells
59104	**HA**	HA	XYPA	MD	Village of Great Elm

Class 59/2. Owned by DB Cargo.

59201 *	**DB**	DB	WDAM	MD	
59202 *	**DB**	DB	WDAM	MD	Alan Meddows Taylor MD Mendip Rail Limited
59203 *	**DB**	DB	WDAM	MD	
59204 *	**DB**	DB	WDAM	MD	
59205 *b	**DB**	DB	WDAM	MD	
59206 *b	**DB**	DB	WDAM	MD	John F. Yeoman Rail Pioneer

CLASS 60　　　BRUSH/MIRRLEES　　　Co-Co

Built: 1989–93 by Brush Traction at Loughborough.
Engine: Mirrlees 8MB275T of 2310 kW (3100 hp) at 1000 rpm.
Main Alternator: Brush BA1006A.
Traction Motors: Brush TM2161A.
Maximum Tractive Effort: 500 kN (106500 lbf).
Continuous Tractive Effort: 336 kN (71570 lbf) at 17.4 mph.
Power at Rail: 1800 kW (2415 hp).　　**Train Brakes:** Air.
Brake Force: 74 t (+ 62 t).　　**Dimensions:** 21.34 × 2.64 m.
Weight: 129 t (+ 131 t).　　**Wheel Diameter:** 1118 mm.
Design Speed: 62 mph.　　**Maximum Speed:** 60 mph.
Fuel Capacity: 4546 (+ 5225) litres.　　**Route Availability:** 8.
Train Supply: Not equipped.

All equipped with Slow Speed Control.

* Refurbished locomotives.

60034, 60064, 60072, 60073, 60077, 60084 and 60090 carry their names on one side only.

60500 originally carried the number 60016.

Advertising liveries: 60066 Powering Drax (silver).

60099 Tata Steel (silver).

60001 *	**DB**	DB	WCAT	TO	
60002 +*	**CS**	CS	COLO	RU	
60003 +	**E**	DB	WQBA	TO (S)	FREIGHT TRANSPORT ASSOCIATION

60004 +	**E**	DB	WQBA	TO (S)	
60005 +	**E**	DB	WQBA	TO (S)	
60006	**CU**	DB	WQBA	TO (S)	
60007 +*	**DB**	DB	WCBT	TO	The Spirit of Tom Kendell
60008	**E**	DB	WQBA	TO (S)	Sir William McAlpine
60009 +	**E**	DB	WQBA	TO (S)	
60010 +*	**DB**	DB	WQAB	TO (S)	
60011	**DB**	DB	WQAB	TO (S)	
60012 +	**E**	DB	WQBA	TO (S)	
60013	**EG**	DB	WQCA	TO (S)	Robert Boyle
60014	**EG**	DB	WQBA	TO (S)	
60015 +*	**DB**	DB	WQAB	TO (S)	
60017 +*	**DB**	DB	WCBT	TO	
60018	**E**	DB	WQBA	TO (S)	
60019 *	**DB**	DB	WCAT	TO	Port of Grimsby & Immingham
60020 +*	**DB**	DB	WCBT	TO	The Willows
60021 +*	**CS**	CS	COLO	RU	
60022 +	**E**	DB	WQBA	TO (S)	
60023 +	**E**	DB	WQBA	TO (S)	
60024 *	**DB**	DB	WQAB	TO (S)	Clitheroe Castle
60025 +	**E**	DB	WQBA	TO (S)	
60026 +*	**CS**	CS	COLO	RU	
60027 +	**E**	DB	WQCA	TO (S)	
60028 +	**EG**	DB	WQCA	CE (S)	
60029	**E**	DB	WQCA	CE (S)	
60030 +	**E**	DB	WQBA	TO (S)	
60031	**E**	DB	WQBA	TO (S)	
60032	**F**	DB	WQBA	TO (S)	
60033 +	**CU**	DB	WQCA	TO (S)	Tees Steel Express
60034	**EG**	DB	WQCA	TO (S)	Carnedd Llewelyn
60035	**E**	DB	WQAB	TO (S)	
60036	**E**	DB	WQBA	TO (S)	GEFCO
60037 +	**E**	DB	WQBA	TO (S)	
60038 +	**E**	DB	WQCA	CE (S)	
60039 *	**DB**	DB	WCAT	TO	Dove Holes
60040 *	**DB**	DB	WCAT	TO	The Territorial Army Centenary
60041 +	**E**	DB	WQCA	TO (S)	
60042	**E**	DB	WQBA	TO (S)	
60043	**E**	DB	WQBA	TO (S)	
60044 *	**DB**	DB	WCAT	TO	Dowlow
60045	**E**	DB	WQAB	TO (S)	The Permanent Way Institution
60046 +	**EG**	DB	WQCA	CE (S)	
60047 *	**CS**	CS	COLO	RU	
60048	**E**	DB	WQCA	TO (S)	
60049	**E**	DB	WQAB	TO (S)	
60050	**E**	DB	WQBA	TO (S)	
60051 +	**E**	DB	WQBA	TO (S)	
60052 +	**E**	DB	WQBA	TO (S)	Glofa Twr – The last deep mine in Wales – Tower Colliery
60053	**E**	DB	WQBA	TO (S)	
60054 +*	**DB**	DB	WCBT	TO	

60055 +	**EG**	DB	WQCA	CE (S)	
60056 +*	**CS**	CS	COLO	RU	
60057	**EG**	DB	WQBA	TO (S)	Adam Smith
60058 +	**E**	DB	WQBA	TO (S)	
60059 +*	**DB**	DB	WCBT	TO	Swinden Dalesman
60060	**EG**	DB	WQBA	TO (S)	
60061	**F**	DB	WQCA	TO (S)	
60062 *	**DB**	DB	WQAB	TO (S)	Stainless Pioneer
60063 *	**DB**	DB	WQAA	TO (S)	
60064 +	**EG**	DB	WQBA	TO (S)	Back Tor
60065	**E**	DB	WQAB	TO (S)	Spirit of JAGUAR
60066 *	**AL**	DB	WCAT	TO	
60067	**EG**	DB	WQBA	TO (S)	
60068	**EG**	DB	WQBA	TO (S)	
60069	**E**	DB	WQBA	TO (S)	Slioch
60070 +	**F**	DB	WQBA	TO (S)	John Loudon McAdam
60071 +	**E**	DB	WQAB	TO (S)	Ribblehead Viaduct
60072	**EG**	DB	WQBA	TO (S)	Cairn Toul
60073	**EG**	DB	WQBA	TO (S)	Cairn Gorm
60074 *	**DB**	DB	WCAT	TO	
60075	**E**	DB	WQBA	TO (S)	
60076 *	**CS**	CS	COLO	RU	Dunbar
60077 +	**EG**	DB	WQBA	TO (S)	Canisp
60078	**ML**	DB	WQBA	TO (S)	
60079 *	**DB**	DB	WQAB	TO (S)	
60080 +	**E**	DB	WQBA	TO (S)	
60081 +	**GW**	DB	WQBA	TO (S)	
60082	**EG**	DB	WQBA	CE (S)	
60083	**E**	DB	WQBA	TO (S)	
60084	**EG**	DB	WQBA	TO (S)	Cross Fell
60085 *	**CS**	CS	COLO	RU	
60086	**EG**	DB	WQBA	TO (S)	
60087 *	**CS**	CS	COLO	RU	CLIC Sargent www.clicsargent.co.uk
60088	**F**	DB	WQBA	TO (S)	
60089 +	**E**	DB	WQBA	TO (S)	
60090 +	**EG**	DB	WQBA	TO (S)	Quinag
60091 +*	**DB**	DB	WCBT	TO	Barry Needham
60092 +*	**DB**	DB	WCBT	TO	
60093	**E**	DB	WQBA	TO (S)	
60094	**E**	DB	WQBA	TO (S)	Rugby Flyer
60095 *	**CS**	CS	COLO	RU	
60096 +*	**CS**	CS	COLO	RU	
60097 +	**E**	DB	WQBA	TO (S)	
60098 +	**E**	DB	WQBA	TO (S)	
60099	**AL**	DB	WQBA	TO (S)	
60100 *	**DD**	DB	WCAT	TO	
60500	**E**	DB	WQBA	TO (S)	

CLASS 66 DETAILS

CLASS 66   GENERAL MOTORS/EMD   Co-Co

Built: 1998–2008 by General Motors/EMD, London, Ontario, Canada (Model JT42CWR (low emission locos Model JT42CWRM)) or 2013–16 by EMD/Progress Rail, Muncie, Indiana (66752–779).
Engine: General Motors 12N-710G3B-EC two stroke of 2385 kW (3200 hp) at 904 rpm (low emission locos General Motors 12N-710G3B-U2 of 2430 kW (3245 hp at 904 rpm).
Main Alternator: General Motors AR8/CA6.
Traction Motors: General Motors D43TR.
Maximum Tractive Effort: 409 kN (92000 lbf).
Continuous Tractive Effort: 260 kN (58390 lbf) at 15.9 mph.
Power at Rail: 1850 kW (2480 hp).   **Train Brakes:** Air.
Brake Force: 68 t.   **Dimensions:** 21.35 x 2.64 m.
Weight: 127 t.   **Wheel Diameter:** 1120 mm.
Design Speed: 87.5 mph.   **Maximum Speed:** 75 mph (unless stated).
Fuel Capacity: 6550 litres (unless stated). **Route Availability:** 7.
Train Supply: Not equipped.

All equipped with Slow Speed Control.

Class 66s previously used in the UK but now in use abroad are listed in section 6 of this book. Some of the DBC 66s moved to France return to Great Britain from time to time for maintenance or operational requirements.

Class 66 delivery dates. The Class 66 design and delivery has evolved over a 18-year period, with more than 400 locomotives delivered. For clarity the delivery dates (by year) for each batch of locos is as follows:

66001–250	EWS (now DB Cargo). 1998–2000 (some now in use in France or Poland).
66301–305	Fastline. 2008. Now used by DRS.
66401–410	DRS. 2003. Now in use with GB Railfreight or Colas Rail and renumbered 66733–737 and 66742–746 (66734 since scrapped).
66411–420	DRS. 2006. Now leased by Freightliner (66411/412/417 exported to Poland).
66421–430	DRS. 2007
66431–434	DRS. 2008
66501–505	Freightliner. 1999
66506–520	Freightliner. 2000
66521–525	Freightliner. 2000 (66521 since scrapped).
66526–531	Freightliner. 2001
66532–537	Freightliner. 2001
66538–543	Freightliner. 2001
66544–553	Freightliner. 2001
66554	Freightliner. 2002†
66555–566	Freightliner. 2002
66567–574	Freightliner. 2003. 66573–574 now used by Colas Rail and renumbered 66846–847.
66575–577	Freightliner. 2004. Now used by Colas Rail and renumbered 66848–850.
66578–581	Freightliner. 2005. Now used by GBRf and renumbered 66738–741.

66582–594	Freightliner. 2007 (66582/583/584/586 exported to Poland).
66595–599	Freightliner. 2008
66601–606	Freightliner. 2000
66607–612	Freightliner. 2002 (66607/609/611/612 exported to Poland)
66613–618	Freightliner. 2003
66619–622	Freightliner. 2005
66623–625	Freightliner. 2007 (66624/625 exported to Poland).
66701–707	GB Railfreight. 2001
66708–712	GB Railfreight. 2002
66713–717	GB Railfreight. 2003
66718–722	GB Railfreight. 2006
66723–727	GB Railfreight. 2006
66728–732	GB Railfreight. 2008
66747–749	Built in 2008 as 20078968-004/006/007 (DE 6313/15/16) for Crossrail AG in the Netherlands but never used. Sold to GB Railfreight in 2012.
66750–751	Built in 2003 as 20038513-01/04 and have worked in the Netherlands, Germany and Poland. GBRf secured these two locomotives on lease in 2013.
66752–772	GB Railfreight. 2014.
66773–779	GB Railfreight. 2016.
66951–952	Freightliner. 2004
66953–957	Freightliner. 2008

† Replacement for 66521, written off in the Great Heck accident in 2001.

Class 66/0. DB Cargo-operated locos.

All fitted with Swinghead Automatic "Buckeye" Combination Couplers except 66001 and 66002.

† Fitted with additional lights and drawgear for Lickey banking duties.

t Fitted with tripcocks for working over London Underground tracks between Harrow-on-the-Hill and Amersham.

66001 t	**DB**	DB	WBAT	TO
66002	**E**	DB	WBAT	TO
66003	**E**	DB	WBAT	TO
66004	**E**	DB	WBAE	TO
66005	**E**	DB	WBAT	TO
66006	**E**	DB	WBAT	TO
66007	**E**	DB	WBAR	TO
66008	**E**	DB	WQAB	TO (S)
66009	**E**	DB	WBAE	TO
66011	**E**	DB	WBAE	TO
66012	**E**	DB	WBAT	TO
66013	**E**	DB	WBAE	TO
66014	**E**	DB	WBAE	TO
66015	**E**	DB	WBAE	TO
66016	**E**	DB	WBAE	TO
66017 t	**E**	DB	WBTT	TO
66018	**E**	DB	WBAT	TO
66019 t	**E**	DB	WBTT	TO

66020	E	DB	WBAT	TO	
66021	E	DB	WBAR	TO	
66023	E	DB	WBAT	TO	
66024	E	DB	WBAE	TO	
66025	E	DB	WBAE	TO	
66027	E	DB	WBAT	TO	
66030	E	DB	WBAR	TO	
66031	E	DB	WBAT	TO	
66034	E	DB	WBAT	TO	
66035	E	DB	WBAT	TO	
66037	E	DB	WBAE	TO	
66039	E	DB	WBAE	TO	
66040	E	DB	WBAR	TO	
66041	E	DB	WBAT	TO	
66043	E	DB	WBAE	TO	
66044	E	DB	WBAE	TO	
66046	E	DB	WQAB	TO (S)	
66047	E	DB	WBAT	TO	
66050	E	DB	WBAE	TO	EWS Energy
66051	E	DB	WBAR	TO	
66053	E	DB	WBAT	TO	
66054	E	DB	WBAR	TO	
66055 †	DB	DB	WBAR	TO	Alain Thauvette
66056 †	E	DB	WBLT	TO	
66057 †	E	DB	WBLT	TO	
66058 †	DB	DB	WBLT	TO	Derek Clark
66059 †	E	DB	WBLE	TO	
66060	E	DB	WBAT	TO	
66061	E	DB	WBAE	TO	
66063	E	DB	WBAT	TO	
66065	E	DB	WBAR	TO	
66066	DB	DB	WBAR	TO	Geoff Spencer
66067	E	DB	WBAR	TO	
66068	E	DB	WBAT	TO	
66069	E	DB	WBAR	TO	
66070	E	DB	WBAT	TO	
66074	E	DB	WBAE	TO	
66075	E	DB	WBAT	TO	
66076	E	DB	WBAT	TO	
66077	E	DB	WBAE	TO	
66078	E	DB	WBAT	TO	
66079	E	DB	WBAR	TO	James Nightall G.C.
66080	E	DB	WBAE	TO	
66081	E	DB	WQAB	TO (S)	
66082	E	DB	WBAT	TO	
66083	E	DB	WBAR	TO	
66084	E	DB	WBAT	TO	
66085	E	DB	WBAR	TO	
66086	E	DB	WBAT	TO	
66087	E	DB	WBAT	TO	
66088	E	DB	WBAT	TO	

66089	E	DB	WBAR	TO
66090	E	DB	WBAT	TO
66091	E	DB	WBAE	TO
66092	E	DB	WBAE	TO
66093	E	DB	WBAT	TO
66094	E	DB	WBAE	TO
66095	E	DB	WBAE	TO
66096	E	DB	WBAE	TO
66097	DB	DB	WBAE	TO
66098	E	DB	WBAT	TO
66099 r	E	DB	WBBE	TO
66100 r	E	DB	WBBE	TO
66101 r	DB	DB	WBBT	TO
66102 r	E	DB	WBBE	TO
66103 r	E	DB	WBBE	TO
66104 r	E	DB	WBAR	TO
66105 r	E	DB	WBBE	TO
66106 r	E	DB	WBBT	TO
66107 r	E	DB	WBAR	TO
66108 r	E	DB	WBBT	TO
66109	E	DB	WBAR	TO
66110 r	E	DB	WBBE	TO
66111 r	E	DB	WBBT	TO
66112 r	E	DB	WBBE	TO
66113 r	E	DB	WBBE	TO
66114 r	DB	DB	WBBT	TO
66115	E	DB	WBAT	TO
66116	E	DB	WBAE	TO
66117	E	DB	WBAT	TO
66118	DB	DB	WBAE	TO
66119	E	DB	WBAE	TO
66120	E	DB	WBAE	TO
66121	E	DB	WBAE	TO
66122	E	DB	WBAE	TO
66124	E	DB	WBAT	TO
66125	E	DB	WBAT	TO
66126	E	DB	WBAE	TO
66127	E	DB	WBAT	TO
66128	E	DB	WBAE	TO
66129	E	DB	WBAE	TO
66130	E	DB	WBAT	TO
66131	E	DB	WBAE	TO
66132	E	DB	WBAE	TO
66133	E	DB	WBAE	TO
66134	E	DB	WBAE	TO
66135	E	DB	WBAE	TO
66136	E	DB	WBAT	TO
66137	E	DB	WBAE	TO
66138	E	DB	WBAE	TO
66139	E	DB	WBAE	TO
66140	E	DB	WBAT	TO

Number			Depot	Status	Name
66141	E	DB	WQAB	TO (S)	
66142	E	DB	WBAE	TO	
66143	E	DB	WBAE	TO	
66144	E	DB	WBAR	TO	
66145	E	DB	WBAE	TO	
66147	E	DB	WBAT	TO	
66148	E	DB	WBAT	TO	
66149	E	DB	WBAE	TO	
66150	E	DB	WBAT	TO	
66151	E	DB	WBAE	TO	
66152	**DB**	DB	WBAT	TO	Derek Holmes Railway Operator
66154	E	DB	WBAE	TO	
66155	E	DB	WBAT	TO	
66156	E	DB	WBAE	TO	
66158	E	DB	WBAE	TO	
66160	E	DB	WBAE	TO	
66161	E	DB	WBAE	TO	
66162	E	DB	WBAE	TO	
66164	E	DB	WBAT	TO	
66165	E	DB	WBAR	TO	
66167	E	DB	WBAE	TO	
66168	E	DB	WBAR	TO	
66169	E	DB	WBAT	TO	
66170	E	DB	WBAT	TO	
66171	E	DB	WBAT	TO	
66172	E	DB	WBAT	TO	PAUL MELLENEY
66174	E	DB	WBAE	TO	
66175	E	DB	WBAE	TO	
66176	E	DB	WBAE	TO	
66177	E	DB	WBAT	TO	
66181	E	DB	WBAT	TO	
66182	E	DB	WBAE	TO	
66183	E	DB	WBAE	TO	
66184	E	DB	WBAT	TO	
66185	**DB**	DB	WBAE	TO	DP WORLD London Gateway
66186	E	DB	WBAT	TO	
66187	E	DB	WBAE	TO	
66188	E	DB	WBAR	TO	
66192	E	DB	WBAE	TO	
66193	E	DB	WGEA	TO (S)	
66194	E	DB	WBAR	TO	
66197	E	DB	WBAE	TO	
66198	E	DB	WBAR	TO	
66199	E	DB	WBAE	TO	
66200	E	DB	WBAE	TO	
66201	E	DB	WGEA	TO (S)	
66204	E	DB	WGEA	TO (S)	
66206	E	DB	WBAR	TO	
66207	E	DB	WBAE	TO	
66213	E	DB	WGEA	TO (S)	
66221	E	DB	WBAT	TO	

66230	**E**	DB	WBAT	TO
66232	**E**	DB	WGEA	TO (S)
66238	**E**	DB	WBAR	TO
66250	**E**	DB	WBAE	TO

Class 66/3. Former Fastline-operated locos now operated by DRS. Low emission. Details as Class 66/0 except:

Engine: EMD 12N-710G3B-U2 two stroke of 2420 kW (3245 hp) at 904 rpm.
Traction Motors: General Motors D43TRC.
Fuel Capacity: 5150 litres.

66301	**DS**	BN	XHIM	KM
66302	**DR**	BN	XHIM	KM
66303	**DS**	BN	XHIM	KM
66304	**DS**	BN	XHIM	KM
66305	**DR**	BN	XHIM	KM

66413–434. Low emission. Macquarie Group-owned. Details as Class 66/3.

66413	**DS**	MQ	DFHJ	LD
66414	**FH**	MQ	DFIN	LD
66415	**DS**	MQ	DFHJ	LD
66416	**FH**	MQ	DFIN	LD
66418	**FH**	MQ	DFIN	LD
66419	**DS**	MQ	DFHJ	LD
66420	**FH**	MQ	DFIN	LD
66421	**DR**	MQ	XHIM	KM
66422	**DR**	MQ	XHIM	KM
66423	**DR**	MQ	XHIM	KM
66424	**DR**	MQ	XHIM	KM
66425	**DR**	MQ	XHIM	KM
66426	**DR**	MQ	XHIM	KM
66427	**DR**	MQ	XHIM	KM
66428	**DS**	MQ	XHIM	ZN (S)
66429	**DR**	MQ	XHIM	KM
66430	**DR**	MQ	XHIM	KM
66431	**DR**	MQ	XHIM	KM
66432	**DR**	MQ	XHIM	KM
66433	**DR**	MQ	XHIM	KM
66434	**DR**	MQ	XHIM	KM

Class 66/5. Freightliner-operated locos. Details as Class 66/0.

Advertising livery: 66522 Shanks Waste (one half of loco Freightliner green and one half Shanks' Waste light green).

66501	**FL**	P	DFIM	LD	Japan 2001
66502	**FL**	P	DFIM	LD	Basford Hall Centenary 2001
66503	**FL**	P	DFIM	LD	The RAILWAY MAGAZINE
66504	**FH**	P	DFIM	LD	
66505	**FL**	P	DFIM	LD	
66506	**FL**	E	DFHH	LD	Crewe Regeneration
66507	**FL**	E	DFHJ	LD	
66508	**FL**	E	DFHJ	LD	

Number	Op	Ow	Pool	Depot	Name
66509	FL	E	DFHH	LD	
66510	FL	E	DFHJ	LD	
66511	FL	E	DFHJ	LD	
66512	FL	E	DFHH	LD	
66513	FL	E	DFHJ	LD	
66514	FL	E	DFHJ	LD	
66515	FL	E	DFHJ	LD	
66516	FL	E	DFIM	LD	
66517	FL	E	DFIM	LD	
66518	FL	E	DFHJ	LD	
66519	FL	E	DFHH	LD	
66520	FL	E	DFHH	LD	
66522	AL	E	DFHH	LD	
66523	FL	P	DFHH	LD	
66524	FL	E	DFHJ	LD	
66525	FL	E	DFHJ	LD	
66526	FL	P	DFHJ	LD	Driver Steve Dunn (George)
66528	FH	P	DFHH	LD	Madge Elliot MBE Borders Railway Opening 2015
66529	FL	P	DFHH	LD	
66531	FL	P	DFHJ	LD	
66532	FL	P	DFIM	LD	P&O Nedlloyd Atlas
66533	FL	P	DFIM	LD	Hanjin Express/Senator Express
66534	FL	P	DFIM	LD	OOCL Express
66536	FL	P	DFHJ	LD	
66537	FL	P	DFIM	LD	
66538	FL	E	DFIM	LD	
66539	FL	E	DFHH	LD	
66540	FL	E	DFIM	LD	Ruby
66541	FL	E	DFIM	LD	
66542	FL	E	DFIM	LD	
66543	FL	E	DFIM	LD	
66544	FL	P	DFHJ	LD	
66545	FL	P	DFHH	LD	
66546	FL	P	DFHH	LD	
66547	FL	P	DFHH	LD	
66548	FL	P	DFHH	LD	
66549	FL	P	DFHH	LD	
66550	FL	P	DFHH	LD	
66551	FL	P	DFHJ	LD	
66552	FL	P	DFHH	LD	Maltby Raider
66553	FL	P	DFHH	LD	
66554	FL	E	DFHH	LD	
66555	FL	E	DFHH	LD	
66556	FL	E	DFIM	LD	
66557	FL	E	DFIM	LD	
66558	FL	E	DFIM	LD	
66559	FL	E	DFHH	LD	
66560	FL	E	DFHH	LD	
66561	FL	E	DFHH	LD	
66562	FL	E	DFHH	LD	

66563	**FL**	E	DFHJ	LD	
66564	**FL**	E	DFHJ	LD	
66565	**FL**	E	DFIM	LD	
66566	**FL**	E	DFIM	LD	
66567	**FL**	E	DFIM	LD	
66568	**FL**	E	DFIM	LD	
66569	**FL**	E	DFIM	LD	
66570	**FL**	E	DFIM	LD	
66571	**FL**	E	DFIM	LD	
66572	**FL**	E	DFIM	LD	

Class 66/5. Freightliner-operated low emission locos. Details as Class 66/3.

66585	**FL**	MQ	DFHJ	LD	The Drax Flyer
66587	**FL**	MQ	DFIN	LD	
66588	**FL**	MQ	DFIN	LD	
66589	**FL**	MQ	DFIN	LD	
66590	**FL**	MQ	DFIN	LD	
66591	**FL**	MQ	DFIN	LD	
66592	**FL**	MQ	DFIN	LD	Johnson Stevens Agencies
66593	**FL**	MQ	DFIN	LD	3MG MERSEY MULTIMODAL GATEWAY
66594	**FL**	MQ	DFIN	LD	NYK Spirit of Kyoto
66595	**FL**	BN	DFHJ	LD	
66596	**FL**	BN	DFHJ	LD	
66597	**FL**	BN	DFHJ	LD	Viridor
66598	**FL**	BN	DFHG	LD	
66599	**FL**	BN	DFHG	LD	

Class 66/6. Freightliner-operated locomotives with modified gear ratios. Details as Class 66/0 except:

Maximum Tractive Effort: 467 kN (105080 lbf).
Continuous Tractive Effort: 296 kN (66630 lbf) at 14.0 mph.
Design Speed: 65 mph.   **Maximum Speed:** 65 mph.

66601	**FL**	P	DFHH	LD	The Hope Valley
66602	**FL**	P	DFHH	LD	
66603	**FL**	P	DFHH	LD	
66604	**FL**	P	DFHH	LD	
66605	**FL**	P	DFHH	LD	
66606	**FL**	P	DFHH	LD	
66607	**FL**	P	DFHH	LD	
66610	**FL**	P	DFHH	LD	
66613	**FL**	E	DFHH	LD	
66614	**FL**	E	DFHH	LD	
66615	**FL**	E	DFHH	LD	
66616	**FL**	E	DFHH	LD	
66617	**FL**	E	DFHH	LD	
66618	**FL**	E	DFHH	LD	Railways Illustrated Annual Photographic Awards Alan Barnes
66619	**FL**	E	DFHH	LD	Derek W. Johnson MBE
66620	**FL**	E	DFHH	LD	
66621	**FL**	E	DFHH	LD	

66622–66717

| 66622 | **FL** | E | DFHH | LD | |

Class 66/6. Freightliner-operated low emission loco with modified gear ratios.
Details as Class 66/6 except:

Fuel Capacity: 5150 litres.

Non-standard livery: 66623 Bardon Aggregates blue.

| 66623 | **0** | MQ | DFHG | LD | Bill Bolsover |

Class 66/7. GB Railfreight-operated locos. Details as Class 66/0.

Non-standard/advertising liveries:

66709 MSC – blue with images of a container ship.

66718 London Underground 150, (black).

66720 Day and night (various colours, different on each side).

66721 London Underground 150 (white with tube map images).

66727 Maritime (blue).

66779 BR dark green.

66701	**GB**	E	GBBT	RR	
66702	**GB**	E	GBBT	RR	Blue Lightning
66703	**GB**	E	GBBT	RR	Doncaster PSB 1981–2002
66704	**GB**	E	GBBT	RR	Colchester Power Signalbox
66705	**GB**	E	GBBT	RR	Golden Jubilee
66706	**GB**	E	GBBT	RR	Nene Valley
66707	**GB**	E	GBBT	RR	Sir Sam Fay GREAT CENTRAL RAILWAY
66708	**GB**	E	GBBT	RR	Jayne
66709	**AL**	E	GBBT	RR	Sorrento
66710	**GB**	E	GBBT	RR	Phil Packer BRIT
66711	**AI**	E	GBBT	RR	Sence
66712	**GB**	E	GBBT	RR	Peterborough Power Signalbox
66713	**GB**	E	GBBT	RR	Forest City
66714	**GB**	E	GBBT	RR	Cromer Lifeboat
66715	**GB**	E	GBBT	RR	VALOUR – IN MEMORY OF ALL RAILWAY EMPLOYEES WHO GAVE THEIR LIVES FOR THEIR COUNTRY
66716	**GB**	E	GBBT	RR	LOCOMOTIVE & CARRIAGE INSTITUTION CENTENARY 1911–2011
66717	**GB**	E	GBBT	RR	Good Old Boy

66718–746. Low emission. GB Railfreight locos.

All details as Class 66/0 except 66718–732/747–749 as below:

Engine: EMD 12N-710G3B-U2 two stroke of 2420 kW (3245 hp) at 904 rpm.
Traction Motors: General Motors D43TRC.
Fuel Capacity: 5546 litres (66718–722) or 5150 litres (66723–732/747–749).

66747–749 were originally built for Crossrail AG in the Netherlands.
66750/751 were originally built for mainland Europe in 2003.

66718	**AL**	E	GBLT		RR	Sir Peter Hendy CBE
66719	**GB**	E	GBLT		RR	METRO-LAND
66720	**O**	E	GBLT		RR	
66721	**AL**	E	GBLT		RR	Harry Beck
66722	**GB**	E	GBLT		RR	Sir Edward Watkin
66723	**FS**	E	GBLT		RR	Chinook
66724	**FS**	E	GBLT		RR	Drax Power Station
66725	**FS**	E	GBLT		RR	SUNDERLAND
66726	**FS**	E	GBLT		RR	SHEFFIELD WEDNESDAY
66727	**AL**	E	GBLT		RR	Maritime One
66728	**GB**	P	GBLT		RR	Institution of Railway Operators
66729	**GB**	P	GBLT		RR	DERBY COUNTY
66730	**GB**	P	GBLT		RR	Whitemoor
66731	**GB**	P	GBLT		RR	interhub GB
66732	**GB**	P	GBLT		RR	GBRf The First Decade 1999–2009 John Smith – MD
66733 (66401) r	**GB**	P	GBFM		RR	Cambridge PSB
66735 (66403)	**GB**	P	GBBT		RR	
66736 (66404) r	**GB**	P	GBFM		RR	WOLVERHAMPTON WANDERERS
66737 (66405) r	**GB**	P	GBFM		RR	Lesia
66738 (66578)	**GB**	BN	GBBT		RR	HUDDERSFIELD TOWN
66739 (66579)	**GB**	BN	GBFM		RR	Bluebell Railway
66740 (66580) r	**GB**	BN	GBFM		RR	Sarah
66741 (66581)	**GB**	BN	GBBT		RR	Swanage Railway
66742 (66406, 66841)	**GB**	BN	GBBT		RR	ABP Port of Immingham Centenary 1912–2012
66743 (66407, 66842) r	**M**	BN	GBFM		RR	
66744 (66408, 66843)	**GB**	BN	GBBT		RR	Crossrail
66745 (66409, 66844)	**GB**	BN	GBRT		RR	Modern Railways The first 50 years
66746 (66410, 66845) r	**M**	BN	GBFM		RR	
66747 (20078968-007)	**GB**	GB	GBEB		RR	
66748 (20078968-004)	**GB**	GB	GBEB		RR	West Burton 50
66749 (20078968-006)	**GB**	GB	GBEB		RR	
66750 (20038513-01)	**GB**	GB	GBEB		RR	Bristol Panel Signal Box
66751 (20038513-04) c	**GB**	BN	GBEB		RR	Inspirational Delivered Hitachi Rail Europe

66752–779. Low emission. New build locomotives (66773–779 on order). Details as Class 66/3.

66752	**GB**	GB	GBEL		RR	The Hoosier State
66753	**GB**	GB	GBEL		RR	EMD Roberts Road
66754	**GB**	GB	GBEL		RR	Northampton Saints
66755	**GB**	GB	GBEL		RR	
66756	**GB**	GB	GBEL		RR	
66757	**GB**	GB	GBEL		RR	West Somerset Railway
66758	**GB**	GB	GBEL		RR	
66759	**GB**	GB	GBEL		RR	Chippy
66760	**GB**	GB	GBEL		RR	David Gordon Harris

66761	**GB**	GB	GBEL	RR	Wensleydale Railway Association 25 Years 1990–2015
66762	**GB**	GB	GBEL	RR	
66763	**GB**	GB	GBEL	RR	Severn Valley Railway
66764	**GB**	GB	GBEL	RR	
66765	**GB**	GB	GBEL	RR	
66766	**GB**	GB	GBEL	RR	
66767	**GB**	GB	GBEL	RR	
66768	**GB**	GB	GBEL	RR	
66769	**GB**	GB	GBEL	RR	
66770	**GB**	GB	GBEL	RR	
66771	**GB**	GB	GBEL	RR	
66772	**GB**	GB	GBEL	RR	
66773	**GB**	GB	GBNB	RR	
66774	**GB**	GB	GBNB	RR	
66775	**GB**	GB	GBNB	RR	
66776	**GB**	GB	GBNB	RR	
66777	**GB**	GB	GBNB	RR	
66778	**GB**	GB	GBNB	RR	
66779	**0**	GB	GBEL	RR	EVENING STAR

Class 66/8. Colas Rail locos. Details as Class 66/0.

66846	(66573)	**CS**	CS	COLO	RU	
66847	(66574)	**CS**	CS	COLO	RU	
66848	(66575)	**CS**	CS	COLO	RU	
66849	(66576)	**CS**	CS	COLO	RU	Wylam Dilly
66850	(66577)	**CS**	CS	COLO	RU	David Maidment OBE

Class 66/9. Freightliner locos. Low emission "demonstrator" locos. Details as Class 66/3.

* **Fuel Capacity:** 5905 litres.

66951	*	**FL**	E	DFHG	LD
66952		**FL**	E	DFHG	LD

Class 66/9. Freightliner-operated low emission locos. Owing to the 665xx number range being full, subsequent deliveries of 66/5s were numbered from 66953 onwards. Details as Class 66/5 (low emission).

66953	**FL**	BN	DFHJ	LD	
66954	**FL**	BN	DFIN	LD	
66955	**FL**	BN	DFIN	LD	
66956	**FL**	BN	DFHG	LD	
66957	**FL**	BN	DFHG	LD	Stephenson Locomotive Society 1909–2009

CLASS 67　ALSTOM/GENERAL MOTORS EMD Bo-Bo

Built: 1999–2000 by Alstom at Valencia, Spain, as sub-contractors for General Motors (General Motors model JT42 HW-HS).
Engine: GM 12N-710G3B-EC two stroke of 2385 kW (3200 hp) at 904 rpm.
Main Alternator: General Motors AR9A/HEP7/CA6C.
Traction Motors: General Motors D43FM.
Maximum Tractive Effort: 141 kN (31770 lbf).
Continuous Tractive Effort: 90 kN (20200 lbf) at 46.5 mph.
Power at Rail: 1860 kW.　**Train Brakes:** Air.
Brake Force: 78 t.　**Dimensions:** 19.74 x 2.72 m.
Weight: 90 t.　**Wheel Diameter:** 965 mm.
Design Speed: 125 mph.　**Maximum Speed:** 125 mph.
Fuel Capacity: 4927 litres.　**Route Availability:** 8.
Train Supply: Electric, index 66.

All equipped with Slow Speed Control and Swinghead Automatic "Buckeye" Combination Couplers.

67001/002/003/014/022/029 have been modified to operate in push-pull mode on the Arriva Trains Wales loco-hauled sets.

67004, 67007, 67009 and 67011 were fitted with cast iron brake blocks for working the Fort William Sleeper. **Maximum Speed:** 80 mph.

Non-standard liveries:

67026 Diamond Jubilee silver.

67029 All over silver with DB logos.

67001	**AB**	DB	WQAA	CE (S)
67002	**AB**	DB	WAWC	CE
67003	**AB**	DB	WAWC	CE
67004 r	**CA**	DB	WQAB	CE (S) Cairn Gorm
67005	**RZ**	DB	WAAC	CE Queen's Messenger
67006	**RZ**	DB	WAAC	CE Royal Sovereign
67007 r	**E**	DB	WABC	CE
67008	**E**	DB	WAAC	CE
67009 r	**E**	DB	WABC	CE
67010	**DB**	DB	WAAC	CE
67011 r	**E**	DB	WQAB	CE (S)
67012	**CM**	DB	WAAC	CE
67013	**DB**	DB	WAWC	CE
67014	**CM**	DB	WAAC	CE
67015	**DB**	DB	WAAC	CE
67016	**E**	DB	WAAC	CE
67017	**E**	DB	WQAB	CE (S) Arrow
67010	**DD**	DB	WAAC	CE Keith Heller
67019	**E**	DB	WQBA	CE (S)
67020	**E**	DB	WQAB	CE (S)
67021	**E**	DB	WAAC	CE
67022	**E**	DB	WAWC	CE
67023	**E**	DB	WQAA	CE (S)

67024	E	DB	WAAC	CE	
67025	E	DB	WQBA	CE (S)	Western Star
67026	0	DB	WQAB	CE (S)	Diamond Jubilee
67027	DB	DB	WQBA	CE (S)	
67028	E	DB	WAAC	CE	
67029	0	DB	WAAC	CE	Royal Diamond
67030 r	E	DB	WABC	CE	

CLASS 68　　　　VOSSLOH/STADLER　　　　Bo-Bo

New Vossloh/Stadler mixed-traffic locos currently being delivered to DRS. 68026–032 are on order for delivery in 2017.

Built: 2012–16 by Vossloh/Stadler, Valencia, Spain.
Engine: Caterpillar C175-16 of 2800 kW (3750 hp) at 1740 rpm.
Main Alternator: ABB WGX560.
Traction Motors: 4 x AC frame mounted ABB 4FRA6063.
Maximum Tractive Effort: 317 kN (71260 lbf).
Continuous Tractive Effort:
Power at Rail:
Brake Force: 73 t.
Weight: 85 t.
Design Speed: 100 mph.
Fuel Capacity: 6000 litres.
Train Supply: Electric, index 96.
Train Brakes: Air.
Dimensions: 20.50 x 2.69 m.
Wheel Diameter: 1100 mm.
Maximum Speed: 100 mph.
Route Availability: 7.

68008–015 have been modified to operate in push-pull mode on the Chiltern Railways loco-hauled sets.

68001	DI	BN	XHVE	CR	Evolution
68002	DI	BN	XHVE	CR	Intrepid
68003	DI	BN	XHVE	CR	Astute
68004	DI	BN	XHVE	CR	Rapid
68005	DI	BN	XHVE	CR	Defiant
68006	SR	BN	XHVE	CR	Daring
68007	SR	BN	XHVE	CR	Valiant
68008	DI	BN	XHVE	CR	Avenger
68009	DI	BN	XHVE	CR	Titan
68010	CM	BN	XHCE	CR	
68011	CM	BN	XHCE	CR	
68012	CM	BN	XHCE	CR	
68013	CM	BN	XHCE	CR	
68014	CM	BN	XHCE	CR	
68015	CM	BN	XHCE	CR	
68016	DI	BN	XHVE	CR	Fearless
68017	DI	BN	XHVE	CR	Hornet
68018	DI	BN	XHVE	CR	Vigilant
68019	DI	BN	XHVE	CR	Brutus
68020	DI	BN	XHVE	CR	Reliance
68021	DI	BN	XHVE	CR	Tireless

68022	**DI**	BN	XHVE	CR	Resolution
68023	**DI**	BN	XHVE	CR	Achilles
68024	**DI**	BN	XHVE	CR	Centaur
68025	**DI**	BN	XHVE	CR	Superb
68026		BN			
68027		BN			
68028		BN			
68029		BN			
68030		BN			
68031		BN			
68032		BN			

CLASS 70 GENERAL ELECTRIC Co-Co

New GE "PowerHaul" locomotives. 70012 was badly damaged whilst being unloaded in 2011 and was returned to Pennsylvania.

70801 (built as 70099) is a Turkish-built demonstrator that arrived in Britain in October 2012. Colas Rail leased this locomotive and then in 2013 ordered a further nine locomotives (70802–810) that were delivered in 2014.

70811–817 are on order for delivery in 2017.

Built: 2009–17 by General Electric, Erie, Pennsylvania, USA or by TÜLOMSAS, Eskişehir, Turkey (70801).
Engine: General Electric PowerHaul P616LDA1 of 2848 kW (3820 hp) at 1500 rpm.
Main Alternator: General Electric GTA series.
Traction Motors: AC-GE 5GEB30.
Maximum Tractive Effort: 544 kN (122000 lbf).
Continuous Tractive Effort: 427 kN (96000 lbf) at ?? mph.
Power at Rail:
Brake Force: 96.7 t.
Weight: 129 t.
Design Speed: 75 mph.
Fuel Capacity: 6000 litres.
Train Supply: Not equipped.
Train Brakes: Air.
Dimensions: 21.71 x 2.64 m.
Wheel Diameter: 1066 mm.
Maximum Speed: 75 mph.
Route Availability: 7.

Class 70/0. Freightliner locomotives.

70001	**FH**	MQ	DFGI	LD	PowerHaul
70002	**FH**	MQ	DFGH	LD	
70003	**FH**	MQ	DFGH	LD	
70004	**FH**	MQ	DFGH	LD	The Coal Industry Society
70005	**FH**	MQ	DFGH	LD	
70006	**FH**	MQ	DFGH	LD	
70007	**FH**	MQ	DFGI	LD	
70008	**FH**	MQ	DFGI	LD	
70009	**FH**	MQ	DFGI	LD	
70010	**FH**	MQ	DFGI	LD	
70011	**FH**	MQ	DFGI	LD	

70013	**FH**	MQ	DFGI	LD
70014	**FH**	MQ	DFGI	LD
70015	**FH**	MQ	DFGI	LD
70016	**FH**	MQ	DFGI	LD
70017	**FH**	MQ	DFGI	LD
70018	**FH**	MQ	DFGI	LD
70019	**FH**	MQ	DFGI	LD
70020	**FH**	MQ	DFGI	LD

Class 70/8. Colas Rail locomotives. 70811–817 are on order.

70801	**CS**	LF	COLO	RU
70802	**CS**	LF	COLO	RU
70803	**CS**	LF	COLS	LA (S)
70804	**CS**	LF	COLO	RU
70805	**CS**	LF	COLO	RU
70806	**CS**	LF	COLO	RU
70807	**CS**	LF	COLO	RU
70808	**CS**	LF	COLO	RU
70809	**CS**	LF	COLO	RU
70810	**CS**	LF	COLO	RU

70811
70812
70813
70814
70815
70816
70817

2. ELECTRO-DIESEL & ELECTRIC LOCOMOTIVES

CLASS 73/1   BR/ENGLISH ELECTRIC   Bo-Bo

Electro-diesel locomotives which can operate either from a DC supply or using power from a diesel engine.

Built: 1965–67 by English Electric Co. at Vulcan Foundry, Newton-le-Willows.
Engine: English Electric 4SRKT of 447 kW (600 hp) at 850 rpm.
Main Generator: English Electric 824/5D.
Electric Supply System: 750 V DC from third rail.
Traction Motors: English Electric 546/1B.
Maximum Tractive Effort (Electric): 179 kN (40000 lbf).
Maximum Tractive Effort (Diesel): 160 kN (36000 lbf).
Continuous Rating (Electric): 1060 kW (1420 hp) giving a tractive effort of 35 kN (7800 lbf) at 68 mph.
Continuous Tractive Effort (Diesel): 60 kN (13600 lbf) at 11.5 mph.
Maximum Rail Power (Electric): 2350 kW (3150 hp) at 42 mph.
Train Brakes: Air, vacuum & electro-pneumatic († Air & electro-pneumatic).
Brake Force: 31 t.   **Dimensions:** 16.36 x 2.64 m.
Weight: 77 t.   **Wheel Diameter:** 1016 mm.
Design Speed: 90 mph.   **Maximum Speed:** 90 mph.
Fuel Capacity: 1409 litres.   **Route Availability:** 6.
Train Supply: Electric, index 66 (on electric power only).

Formerly numbered E6001–E6020/E6022–E6026/E6028–E6049 (not in order).

Locomotives numbered in the 732xx series are classed as 73/2 and were originally dedicated to Gatwick Express services.

There have been two separate Class 73 rebuild projects. For GB Railfreight 11 locomotives were rebuilt at Brush, Loughborough with a 1600 hp MTU engine (these were renumbered in the 73961–971 series). For Network Rail 73104/211 were rebuilt at RVEL Derby (now LORAM) with a pair of QSK19 750 hp engines (these have been renumbered 73951/952).

Non-standard liveries:

73128 Two-tone grey.
73139 Light blue & light grey.

73101	**PC**	LO	RVEL	ZA (S)	
73107	**GB**	GB	GBED	SE	Tracy
73109	**GB**	GB	GBED	SE	
73110	**CB**	GB	GBED	SE	Borough of Eastleigh
73128	**GB**	GB	GBED	SE	O.V.S. BULLEID C.B.E.
73133	**TT**	TT	MBED	BM	
73134	**IC**	GB	GBBR	LB (S)	Woking Homes 1885–1985
73136	**GB**	GB	GBED	SE	Mhairi
73138	**Y**	NR	QADD	ZA	

73139	**0**	LO	RVLO	ZA (S)		
73141	**GB**	GB	GBED	SE	Charlotte	
73201 †	**B**	GB	GBED	SE	Broadlands	
73202 †	**SN**	P	MBED	SL	Graham Stenning	
73212 †	**GB**	GB	GBED	SE	Fiona	
73213 †	**GB**	GB	GBED	SE	Rhodalyn	
73235 †	**SD**	P	HYWD	BM		

CLASS 73/9 (RVEL) BR/RVEL Bo-Bo

The 7395x number series is reserved for rebuilt Network Rail locomotives.

Rebuilt: Re-engineered by RVEL Derby 2013–15.
Engine: 2 x QSK19 of 560 kW (750 hp) at 1800 rpm (total 1120 kw (1500 hp)).
Main Alternator: 2 x Marathon Magnaplus.
Electric Supply System: 750 V DC from third rail.
Traction Motors: English Electric 546/1B.
Maximum Tractive Effort (Electric): 179 kN (40000 lbf).
Maximum Tractive Effort (Diesel): 179 kN (40000 lbf).
Continuous Rating (Electric): 1060 kW (1420 hp) giving a tractive effort of 35 kN (7800 lbf) at 68 mph.
Continuous Tractive Effort (Diesel): 990 kW (1328 hp) giving a tractive effort of 33 kN (7420 lbf) at 68 mph.
Maximum Rail Power (Electric): 2350 kW (3150 hp) at 42 mph.
Train Brakes: Air.   **Brake Force:** 31 t.
Weight: 77 t.   **Dimensions:** 16.36 x 2.64 m.
Maximum Speed: 90 mph.   **Wheel Diameter:** 1016 mm.
Fuel Capacity: 2260 litres.   **Route Availability:** 6.
Train Supply: None.

73951	(73104)	**Y**	LO	QADD	ZA	Malcolm Brinded
73952	(73211)	**Y**	LO	QADD	ZA	Janis Kong

CLASS 73/9 (GBRf) BR/BRUSH Bo-Bo

GBRf Class 73s rebuilt at Brush Loughborough. 73961–965 are normally used on Network Rail contracts whilst 73966–971 are used by Caledonian Sleeper on its services between Edinburgh, Inverness, Aberdeen and Fort William.

Rebuilt: Re-engineered by Brush, Loughborough 2014– .
Engine: MTU 8V4000 R43L of 1195 kW (1600 hp) at 1800 rpm.
Main Alternator: Lechmotoren SDV 87.53-12.
Electric Supply System: 750 V DC from third rail (73961–965 only).
Traction Motors: English Electric 546/1B.
Maximum Tractive Effort (Electric): 179 kN (40000 lbf).
Maximum Tractive Effort (Diesel): 179 kN (40000 lbf).
Continuous Rating (Electric): 1060 kW (1420 hp) giving a tractive effort of 35 kN (7800 lbf) at 68 mph.
Continuous Tractive Effort (Diesel): awaited.
Maximum Rail Power (Electric): 2350 kW (3150 hp) at 42 mph.
Train Brakes: Air.   **Brake Force:** 31 t.

Weight: 77 t.
Maximum Speed: 90 mph.
Fuel Capacity: 1409 litres.
Dimensions: 16.36 x 2.64 m.
Wheel Diameter: 1016 mm.
Route Availability: 6.
Train Supply: Electric, index 38 (electric & diesel).

73961	(73209)	**GB**	GB	GBNR	SE	Alison
73962	(73204)	**GB**	GB	GBNR	SE	Dick Mabbutt
73963	(73206)	**GB**	GB	GBNR	SE	Janice
73964	(73205)	**GB**	GB	GBNR	SE	Jeanette
73965	(73208)	**GB**	GB	GBNR	SE	

73966–971 have been rebuilt for Caledonian Sleeper but their third rail electric capability has been retained. They have a higher Train Supply index and a slightly higher fuel capacity. Details as 73961–965 except:
Fuel Capacity: 1509 litres.   **Train Supply:** Electric, index 96.

73005 and 73006 were originally built at Eastleigh Works.

73966	(73005)	**CA**	GB	GBCS	EC
73967	(73006)	**CA**	GB	GBCS	EC
73968	(73117)	**CA**	GB	GBCS	EC
73969	(73105)	**CA**	GB	GBCS	EC
73970	(73103)	**CA**	GB	GBCS	EC
73971	(73207)	**CA**	GB	GBCS	EC

CLASS 86   BR/ENGLISH ELECTRIC   Bo-Bo

Built: 1965–66 by English Electric Co at Vulcan Foundry, Newton-le-Willows or by BR at Doncaster Works.
Electric Supply System: 25 kV AC 50 Hz overhead.
Train Brakes: Air.   **Brake Force:** 40 t.
Dimensions: 17.83 x 2.65 m.   **Weight:** 83–86.8 t.
Route Availability: 6.   **Train Supply:** Electric, index 66.

Formerly numbered E3101–E3200 (not in order).

Class 86s exported for use abroad are listed in section 6 of this book.

Class 86/1. Class 87-type bogies & motors.

Details as above except:
Traction Motors: GEC 412AZ frame mounted.
Maximum Tractive Effort: 258 kN (58000 lbf).
Continuous Rating: 3730 kW (5000 hp) giving a tractive effort of 95 kN (21300 lbf) at 87 mph.
Maximum Rail Power: 5860 kW (7860 hp) at 50.8 mph.
Wheel Diameter: 1150 mm.   **Weight:** 86.8 t.
Design Speed: 110 mph.   **Maximum Speed:** 110 mph.

86101		**CA**	EL	GBCH	WN	Sir William A Stanier FRS

86229–86639

Class 86/2. Standard design rebuilt with resilient wheels & Flexicoil suspension.

Traction Motors: AEI 282BZ axle hung.
Maximum Tractive Effort: 207 kN (46500 lbf).
Continuous Rating: 3010 kW (4040 hp) giving a tractive effort of 85 kN (19200 lbf) at 77.5 mph.
Maximum Rail Power: 4550 kW (6100 hp) at 49.5 mph.
Wheel Diameter: 1156 mm.   **Weight:** 85–86.2 t.
Design Speed: 125 mph.   **Maximum Speed:** 100 mph.

Non-standard livery: 86259 BR "Electric blue". Also carries number E3137.

86229	**V**	FL	EPEX	LM (S)	
86246	**AR**	EP	EPEX	WN (S)	
86251	**V**	FL	EPEX	LM (S)	
86259 x	**O**	PP	MBEL	WN	Les Ross

Class 86/4.

Traction Motors: AEI 282AZ axle hung.
Maximum Tractive Effort: 258 kN (58000 lbf).
Continuous Rating: 2680 kW (3600 hp) giving a tractive effort of 89 kN (20000 lbf) at 67 mph.
Maximum Rail Power: 4400 kW (5900 hp) at 38 mph.
Wheel Diameter: 1156 mm.   **Weight:** 83–83.9 t.
Design Speed: 100 mph.   **Maximum Speed:** 100 mph.

86401	**CA**	EL	GBCH	WN	Mons Meg

Class 86/6. Freightliner-operated locomotives.

86608 was regeared and renumbered 86501 between 2000 and 2016.

Details as Class 86/4 except:

Maximum Speed: 75 mph.   **Train Supply:** Electric, isolated.

86604	**FL**	FL	DFNC	CP
86605	**FL**	FL	DFNC	CP
86607	**FL**	FL	DFNC	CP
86608	**FL**	FL	DFNC	CP
86609	**FL**	FL	DFNC	CP
86610	**FL**	FL	DFNC	CP
86612	**FL**	P	DFNC	CP
86613	**FL**	P	DFNC	CP
86614	**FL**	P	DFNC	CP
86622	**FH**	P	DFNC	CP
86627	**FL**	P	DFNC	CP
86628	**FL**	P	DFNC	CP
86632	**FL**	P	DFNC	CP
86637	**FH**	P	DFNC	CP
86638	**FL**	P	DFNC	CP
86639	**FL**	P	DFNC	CP

CLASS 87   BREL/GEC   Bo-Bo

Built: 1973–75 by BREL at Crewe Works.
Electric Supply System: 25 kV AC 50 Hz overhead.
Traction Motors: GEC G412AZ frame mounted.
Maximum Tractive Effort: 258 kN (58000 lbf).
Continuous Rating: 3730 kW (5000 hp) giving a tractive effort of 95 kN (21300 lbf) at 87 mph.
Maximum Rail Power: 5860 kW (7860 hp) at 50.8 mph.
Train Brakes: Air.   **Brake Force:** 40 t.
Dimensions: 17.83 x 2.65 m.   **Weight:** 83.3 t.
Wheel Diameter: 1150 mm.   **Design Speed:** 110 mph.
Maximum Speed: 110 mph.   **Train Supply:** Electric, index 95.
Route Availability: 6.

Class 87s exported for use abroad are listed in section 6 of this book.

87002   **CA**   EL   GBCH   WN   Royal Sovereign

CLASS 88   VOSSLOH/STADLER   Bo-Bo

Ten new Vossloh/Stadler bi-mode locomotives on order for DRS and due for delivery 2016–17. Full details awaited.
Built: 2015–16 by Vossloh/Sladler, Valencia, Spain.
Electric Supply System: 25 kV AC 50 Hz overhead.
Engine: Caterpillar C27 12-cylinder 708 kW (950 hp) at 1800 rpm.
Traction Motors: ABB.
Maximum Tractive Effort (Electric): 317 kN (71260 lbf).
Maximum Tractive Effort (Diesel): 317 kN (71260 lbf).
Continuous Rating: 4000 kW (5360 hp).
Maximum Rail Power:
Train Brakes: Air, regenerative & rheostatic.
Brake Force: 73 t.   **Dimensions:**
Weight: 85 t.   **Wheel Diameter:** 1100 mm.
Fuel capacity: **Train Supply:** Electric, index 96.
Design Speed: 100 mph.   **Maximum Speed:** 100 mph.
Route Availability: 7.

88001	**DI**	BN
88002	**DI**	BN
88003	**DI**	BN
88004	**DI**	BN
88005	**DI**	BN
88006	**DI**	BN
88007	**DI**	BN
88008	**DI**	BN
88009	**DI**	BN
88010	**DI**	BN

CLASS 90   GEC   Bo-Bo

Built: 1987–90 by BREL at Crewe Works (as sub-contractors for GEC).
Electric Supply System: 25 kV AC 50 Hz overhead.
Traction Motors: GEC G412CY frame mounted.
Maximum Tractive Effort: 258 kN (58000 lbf).
Continuous Rating: 3730 kW (5000 hp) giving a tractive effort of 95 kN (21300 lbf) at 87 mph.
Maximum Rail Power: 5860 kW (7860 hp) at 68.3 mph.
Train Brakes: Air.
Brake Force: 40 t.
Weight: 84.5 t.
Design Speed: 110 mph.
Train Supply: Electric, index 95.
Dimensions: 18.80 x 2.74 m.
Wheel Diameter: 1150 mm.
Maximum Speed: 110 mph.
Route Availability: 7.

Advertising livery: 90024 Malcolm Logistics (blue).

90001 b	**GA**	P	IANA	NC	Crown Point
90002 b	**GA**	P	IANA	NC	Eastern Daily Press 1870–2010 SERVING NORFOLK FOR 140 YEARS
90003 b	**GA**	P	IANA	NC	
90004 b	**GA**	P	IANA	NC	City of Chelmsford
90005 b	**GA**	P	IANA	NC	Vice-Admiral Lord Nelson
90006 b	**GA**	P	IANA	NC	Modern Railways Magazine/ Roger Ford
90007 b	**GA**	P	IANA	NC	Sir John Betjeman
90008 b	**GA**	P	IANA	NC	The East Anglian
90009 b	**GA**	P	IANA	NC	
90010 b	**GA**	P	IANA	NC	
90011 b	**GA**	P	IANA	NC	East Anglian Daily Times Suffolk & Proud
90012 b	**GA**	P	IANA	NC	Royal Anglian Regiment
90013 b	**GA**	P	IANA	NC	
90014 b	**GA**	P	IANA	NC	Norfolk and Norwich Festival
90015 b	**GA**	P	IANA	NC	Colchester Castle
90016	**FL**	P	DFLC	CP	
90017	**E**	DB	WQBA	CE (S)	
90018	**DB**	DB	WEAC	CE	The Pride of Bellshill
90019	**DB**	DB	WEAC	CE	Multimodal
90020	**E**	DB	WQAA	CE (S)	Collingwood
90021	**FS**	DB	WQAB	CE (S)	
90022	**EG**	DB	WQBA	CE (S)	Freightconnection
90023	**E**	DB	WQBA	CE (S)	
90024	**AL**	DB	WEAC	CE	
90025	**F**	DB	WQBA	CE (S)	
90026	**E**	DB	WQBA	CE (S)	
90027	**F**	DB	WQBA	CE (S)	Allerton T&RS Depot
90028	**E**	DB	WEAC	CE	
90029	**DB**	DB	WEAC	CE	
90030	**E**	DB	WQBA	CE (S)	
90031	**E**	DB	WQBA	CE (S)	The Railway Children Partnership Working For Street Children Worldwide

90032	**E**	DB	WQBA	CE (S)	
90033	**FE**	DB	WQBA	CE (S)	
90034	**DR**	DB	WEAC	CE	
90035	**E**	DB	WEAC	CE	
90036	**DB**	DB	WEAC	CE	Driver Jack Mills
90037	**E**	DB	WEAC	CE	Spirit of Dagenham
90038	**FE**	DB	WQBA	CE (S)	
90039	**E**	DB	WEAC	CE	
90040	**DB**	DB	WEAC	CE	
90041	**FL**	P	DFLC	CP	
90042	**FH**	P	DFLC	CP	
90043	**FH**	P	DFLC	CP	
90044	**FF**	P	DFLC	CP	
90045	**FH**	P	DFLC	CP	
90046	**FL**	P	DFLC	CP	
90047	**FF**	P	DFLC	CP	
90048	**FF**	P	DFLC	CP	
90049	**FH**	P	DFLC	CP	
90050	**FF**	AV	DHLT	BA (S)	

CLASS 91　　　GEC　　　Bo-Bo

Built: 1988–91 by BREL at Crewe Works (as sub-contractors for GEC).
Electric Supply System: 25 kV AC 50 Hz overhead.
Traction Motors: GEC G426AZ.
Maximum Tractive Effort: 190 kN (43 000 lbf).
Continuous Rating: 4540 kW (6090 hp) giving a tractive effort of 170 kN at 96 mph.
Maximum Rail Power: 4700 kW (6300 hp) at ?? mph.
Train Brakes: Air.
Brake Force: 45 t.
Weight: 84 t.
Design Speed: 140 mph.
Train Supply: Electric, index 95.
Dimensions: 19.41 x 2.74 m.
Wheel Diameter: 1000 mm.
Maximum Speed: 125 mph.
Route Availability: 7.

Locomotives were originally numbered in the 910xx series, but were renumbered upon completion of overhauls at Bombardier, Doncaster by the addition of 100 to their original number. The exception to this rule was 91023 which was renumbered 91132.

91114 has been fitted with a second pantograph for evaluation purposes.

Advertising liveries:

91101 Flying Scotsman (red, white & purple).

91110 Battle of Britain (black and grey).

91111 For the fallen (various with poppy and Union Jack vinyls).

91101	**AL**	E	IECA	BN	FLYING SCOTSMAN
91102	**VE**	E	IECA	BN	City of York
91103	**VE**	E	IECA	BN	
91104	**VE**	E	IECA	BN	
91105	**VE**	E	IECA	BN	
91106	**VE**	E	IECA	BN	
91107	**VE**	E	IECA	BN	SKYFALL
91108	**VE**	E	IECA	BN	
91109	**VE**	E	IECA	BN	Sir Bobby Robson
91110	**AL**	E	IECA	BN	BATTLE OF BRITAIN MEMORIAL FLIGHT
91111	**AL**	E	IECA	BN	For the Fallen
91112	**VE**	E	IECA	BN	
91113	**VE**	E	IECA	BN	
91114	**VE**	E	IECA	BN	Durham Cathedral
91115	**VE**	E	IECA	BN	Blaydon Races
91116	**VE**	E	IECA	BN	
91117	**VE**	E	IECA	BN	WEST RIDING LIMITED
91118	**VE**	E	IECA	BN	
91119	**VE**	E	IECA	BN	
91120	**VE**	E	IECA	BN	
91121	**VE**	E	IECA	BN	
91122	**VE**	E	IECA	BN	
91124	**VE**	E	IECA	BN	
91125	**VE**	E	IECA	BN	
91126	**VE**	E	IECA	BN	
91127	**VE**	E	IECA	BN	
91128	**VE**	E	IECA	BN	INTERCITY 50
91129	**VE**	E	IECA	BN	
91130	**VE**	E	IECA	BN	
91131	**VE**	E	IECA	BN	
91132	**VE**	E	IECA	BN	

CLASS 92   BRUSH   Co-Co

Built: 1993–96 by Brush Traction at Loughborough.
Electric Supply System: 25 kV AC 50 Hz overhead or 750 V DC third rail.
Traction Motors: Asea Brown Boveri design. Model 6FRA 7059B (Asynchronous 3-phase induction motors).
Maximum Tractive Effort: 400 kN (90 000 lbf).
Continuous Rating: 5040 kW (6760 hp) on AC, 4000 kW (5360 hp) on DC.
Maximum Rail Power: **Train Brakes:** Air.
Brake Force: 63 t.   **Dimensions:** 21.34 x 2.67 m.
Weight: 126 t.   **Wheel Diameter:** 1070 mm.
Design Speed: 140 km/h (87 mph).   **Maximum Speed:** 145 km/h (90 mph).
Train Supply: Electric, index 108 (AC), 70 (DC).
Route Availability: 7.

* Modified to operate on High Speed 1.

Class 92s exported for use abroad are listed in section 6 of this book.

Advertising livery: 92017 Stobart Rail (two-tone blue & white).

92004	**EG**	DB	WQBA	CE (S)	Jane Austen
92006	**EP**	GB	GBET	LB (S)	Louis Armand
92007	**EG**	DB	WQBA	CE (S)	Schubert
92008	**EG**	DB	WQBA	CE (S)	Jules Verne
92009 *	**DB**	DB	WQBA	CE (S)	Marco Polo
92010	**CA**	GB	GBST	WN	
92011 *	**EG**	DB	WFBC	CE	Handel
92013	**EG**	DB	WQAA	CE (S)	Puccini
92014	**CA**	GB	GBSL	WN	
92015 *	**DB**	DB	WFBC	CE	
92016 *	**DB**	DB	WFBC	CE	
92017	**AL**	DB	WQBA	CE (S)	Bart the Engine
92018	**CA**	GB	GBST	WN	
92019 *	**EG**	DB	WFBC	CE	Wagner
92020	**EP**	GB	GBET	LB (S)	Milton
92021	**EP**	GB	GBET	CO (S)	Purcell
92022	**EG**	DB	WQBA	CE (S)	Charles Dickens
92023	**CA**	GB	GBST	WN	
92028	**GB**	GB	GBSL	WN	
92029	**EG**	DB	WQBA	CE (S)	Dante
92031 *	**DB**	DB	WQAB	CE (S)	
92032	**GB**	GB	GBST	WN	IMechE Railway Division
92033	**CA**	GB	GBSL	WN	
92035	**EP**	DB	WQBA	CE (S)	Mendelssohn
92036 *	**EG**	DB	WFBC	CE	Bertolt Brecht
92037	**EG**	DB	WQAB	CE (S)	Sullivan
92038	**CA**	GB	GBST	WN	
92040	**EP**	GB	GBET	CO (S)	Goethe
92041 *	**EG**	DB	WQAA	CE (S)	Vaughan Williams
92042 *	**DB**	DB	WFBC	CE	
92043	**EP**	GB	GBST	WN	Debussy
92044	**EP**	GB	GBST	WN	Couperin
92045	**EP**	GB	GBET	LB (S)	Chaucer
92046	**EP**	GB	GBET	LB (S)	Sweelinck

3. EUROTUNNEL LOCOMOTIVES

DIESEL LOCOMOTIVES

0001–0007　　MaK　　　　　　　　　　　　　　Bo-Bo

Channel Tunnel maintenance and rescue train locomotives.
Built: 1991–92 by MaK at Kiel, Germany (Model DE1004).
Engine: MTU 12V 396 TC13 of 940 kW (1260 hp) at 1800 rpm.
Main Alternator: ABB.　　　　　　**Traction Motors:** ABB.
Maximum Tractive Effort: 305 kN (68600 lbf).
Continuous Tractive Effort: 140 kN (31500 lbf) at 20 mph.
Power At Rail: 750 kW (1012 hp).　**Dimensions:** 14.40 x ?? m.
Brake Force: 120 kN.　　　　　　　**Wheel Diameter:** 1000 mm.
Weight: 82 t.　　　　　　　　　　　**Maximum Speed:** 100 km/h.
Design Speed: 120 km/h.　　　　　**Train Brakes:** Air.
Fuel Capacity: 3500 litres.　　　　　**Multiple Working:** Within class.
Train Supply: Not equipped.　　　　**Signalling System:** TVM430 cab signalling.

Registered on TOPS as 21901–910.

0001	**GY**	ET	CO
0002	**GY**	ET	CO
0003	**GY**	ET	CO
0004	**GY**	ET	CO
0005	**GY**	ET	CO

The following five locomotives have been rebuilt from Netherlands Railways/DB Cargo Nederland 6400 Class. 0006/07 were added to the Eurotunnel fleet in 2011, and 0008–10 in 2016. 0010 is to be deployed for shunting at Fréthun.

0006	(6456)	**GY**	ET	CO
0007	(6457)	**GY**	ET	CO
0008	(6450)	**GY**	ET	CO
0009	(6451)	**GY**	ET	CO
0010	(6447)	**EB**	ET	CO

0031–0042　　HUNSLET/SCHÖMA　　　　　　0-4-0

Built: 1989–90 by Hunslet Engine Company at Leeds as 900 mm gauge.
Rebuilt: 1993–94 by Schöma in Germany to 1435 mm gauge.
Engine: Deutz FL10L 413FW of 170 kW (230 hp) at 2300 rpm.
Transmission: Mechanical Clark 5000 series.
Maximum Tractive Effort:
Continuous Tractive Effort:
Power At Rail:
Brake Force:　　　　　　　　　　　**Dimensions:** 6.63 x 2.69 m.
Weight: 26–28 t.　　　　　　　　　**Wheel Diameter:**

Design Speed: 48 km/h.
Fuel Capacity:
Train Supply: Not equipped.
Maximum Speed: 50 km/h.
Train Brakes: Air.
Multiple Working: Not equipped.

* Rebuilt with inspection platforms to check overhead catenary.

0031		**GY**	ET CO	FRANCES
0032		**GY**	ET CO	ELISABETH
0033		**GY**	ET CO	SILKE
0034		**GY**	ET CO	AMANDA
0035		**GY**	ET CO	MARY
0036		**GY**	ET CO	LAURENCE
0037		**GY**	ET CO	LYDIE
0038		**GY**	ET CO	JENNY
0039	*	**GY**	ET CO	PACITA
0040		**GY**	ET CO	JILL
0041	*	**GY**	ET CO	KIM
0042		**GY**	ET CO	NICOLE

ELECTRIC LOCOMOTIVES

9005–9840   BRUSH/ABB   Bo-Bo-Bo

Built: 1993–2002 by Brush Traction at Loughborough.
Supply System: 25 kV AC 50 Hz overhead.
Traction Motors: Asea Brown Boveri design. Asynchronous 3-phase motors. Model 6FHA 7059 (as built). Model 6FHA 7059C (7000 kW rated locos).
Maximum Tractive Effort: 400kN (90 000 lbf).
Continuous Rating: Class 9/0 and 9/1: 5760 kW (7725 hp). Class 9/7 and 9/8: 7000 kW (9387 hp).
Maximum Rail Power:
Brake Force: 50 t.
Weight: 136 t.
Design Speed: 100 mph.
Train Supply: Electric.
Multiple Working: TDM system.
Dimensions: 22.01 x 2.97 x 4.20 m.
Wheel Diameter: 1250 mm.
Maximum Speed: 100 mph.
Train Brakes: Air.

Class 9/0 Original build locos. Built 1993–94.

9005	**EB**	ET CO	JESSYE NORMAN
9007	**EB**	ET CO	DAME JOAN SUTHERLAND
9011	**EB**	ET CO	JOSÉ VAN DAM
9013	**EB**	ET CO	MARIA CALLAS
9015	**EB**	ET CO	LÖTSCHBERG 1913
9018	**EB**	ET CO	WILHELMENIA FERNANDEZ
9022	**EB**	ET CO	DAME JANET BAKER
9024	**EB**	ET CO	GOTTHARD 1882
9026	**EB**	ET CO	FURKATUNNEL 1982
9029	**EB**	ET CO	THOMAS ALLEN
9033	**EB**	ET CO	MONTSERRAT CABALLE
9036	**EB**	ET CO	ALAIN FONDARY
9037	**EB**	ET CO	GABRIEL BACQUIER

▲ Colas Rail-liveried 60096 passes Loughborough with 6E38 13.54 Colnbrook–Lindsey discharged oil tanks on 12/08/16. **Paul Biggs**

▼ DB Cargo-liveried 66101 passes Cossington on the Midland Main Line with 6M45 14.17 Barham–Mountsorrel empty aggregates on 21/05/15. **Paul Biggs**

▲ GB Railfreight-liveried 66717 passes Enterkinfoot on the G&SW line with 6H97 12.35 Hunterston–Drax coal on 14/03/16. **Robin Ralston**

▲ Royal Train-liveried 67006 is seen near Swanley with the 10.14 London Victoria–Folkestone West on 08/05/16. **Jamie Squibbs**

▼ Chiltern Mainline-liveried 68014 passes Neasden with the 17.15 London Marylebone–Kidderminster on 05/07/16. **Robert Pritchard**

▲ Colas Rail-liveried 70807 hauls 6C97 16.46 Westbury–St Austell on the approaches to Tiverton Parkway on 18/05/16. **Stephen Ginn**

▼ GBRf-liveried 73961 and 73964 are seen arriving at Great Yarmouth on the rear of the GB15 railtour on 09/09/16. **Dave Gommersall**

▲ Freightliner-liveried 86639 and 86605 haul 4S88 Felixstowe–Coatbridge north at Wandel on the WCML on 22/04/15. **Andi Walshaw**

▼ Caledonian Sleeper-liveried 87002 stands at Liverpool Lime Street after arrival with the "GB15" railtour from Edinburgh on 11/09/16. **Ian Beardsley**

▲ Brand new bi-mode 88002, in Direct Rail Services livery, stands outside Stadler Rail's Valencia factory in Spain in August 2016. DRS has ten of these locomotives on order. **Courtesy DRS**

▼ Abellio Greater Anglia-liveried 90001 passes Stratford on 14/08/16 with the 16.43 Ipswich–London Liverpool Street. **Robert Pritchard**

▲ Virgin Trains East Coast-liveried 91107 passes Colton with the 08.00 London King's Cross–Edinburgh on 19/09/15.
Andrew Mason

▲ Caledonian Sleeper-liveried 92038 is seen near Lanark Junction with 6S51 12.16 Carlisle–Mossend on 30/09/15. **Robin Ralston**

▼ Eurotunnel-liveried 9810 stands at Coquelles depot on 27 February 2014. **David Haydock**

EUROTUNNEL 9701–9840

Class 9/7. Increased power freight shuttle locos. Built 2001–02 (9711–23 built 1998–2001 as 9101–13 and rebuilt as 9711–23 2010–12).

9701	**EB**	ET	CO
9702	**EB**	ET	CO
9703	**EB**	ET	CO
9704	**EB**	ET	CO
9705	**EB**	ET	CO
9706	**EB**	ET	CO
9707	**EB**	ET	CO

9711	(9101)	**EB**	ET	CO
9712	(9102)	**EB**	ET	CO
9713	(9103)	**EB**	ET	CO
9714	(9104)	**EB**	ET	CO
9715	(9105)	**EB**	ET	CO
9716	(9106)	**EB**	ET	CO
9717	(9107)	**EB**	ET	CO
9718	(9108)	**EB**	ET	CO
9719	(9109)	**EB**	ET	CO
9720	(9110)	**EB**	ET	CO
9721	(9111)	**EB**	ET	CO
9722	(9112)	**EB**	ET	CO
9723	(9113)	**EB**	ET	CO

Class 9/8 Locos rebuilt from Class 9/0 by adding 800 to the loco number. Uprated to 7000 kW.

9801	**EB**	ET	CO	LESLEY GARRETT
9802	**EB**	ET	CO	STUART BURROWS
9803	**EB**	ET	CO	BENJAMIN LUXON
9804	**EB**	ET	CO	VICTORIA DE LOS ANGELES
9806	**EB**	ET	CO	REGINE CRESPIN
9808	**EB**	ET	CO	ELISABETH SODERSTROM
9809	**EB**	ET	CO	FRANÇOISE POLLET
9810	**EB**	ET	CO	JEAN-PHILIPPE COURTIS
9812	**EB**	ET	CO	LUCIANO PAVAROTTI
9814	**EB**	ET	CO	LUCIA POPP
9816	**EB**	ET	CO	WILLARD WHITE
9817	**EB**	ET	CO (S)	JOSÉ CARRERAS
9819	**EB**	ET	CO	MARIA EWING
9820	**EB**	ET	CO	NICOLAI GHIAROV
9821	**EB**	ET	CO	TERESA BERGANZA
9823	**EB**	ET	CO	DAME ELISABETH LEGGE-SCHWARZKOPF
9825	**EB**	ET	CO	
9827	**EB**	ET	CO	BARBARA HENDRICKS
9828	**EB**	ET	CO	DAME KIRI TE KANAWA
9831	**EB**	ET	CO	
9832	**EB**	ET	CO	RENATA TEBALDI
9834	**EB**	ET	CO	MIRELLA FRENI
9835	**EB**	ET	CO	NICOLAI GEDDA
9838	**EB**	ET	CO	HILDEGARD BEHRENS
9840	**EB**	ET	CO	

4. FORMER BR MAIN LINE LOCOS IN INDUSTRIAL SERVICE

Former British Rail main line locomotives considered to be in "industrial use" are listed here. These locomotives do not currently have Network Rail engineering acceptance for operation on the national railway network.

Number Other no./name Location

Class 03

03084	HELEN-LOUISE	West Coast Railway Company, Carnforth
03196	JOYCE/GLYNIS	West Coast Railway Company, Carnforth
D2381		West Coast Railway Company, Carnforth

Class 07

D2991 07007 Arlington Fleet Services, Eastleigh Works, Hampshire

Class 08

08220		EMD, Longport Works, Stoke-on-Trent *(on loan from Nottingham Transport Heritage Centre)*
08308	23	PD Ports, Teesport, Grangetown, Middlesbrough
08331		Midland Railway-Butterley, Derbyshire
08375	21	Hanson Cement, Ketton Cement Works, nr Stamford
08389		Celsa Steel UK, Tremorfa Steelworks, Cardiff
08401		Hams Hall Distribution Park, Coleshill, Warwickshire
08411		RSS, Rye Farm, Wishaw, Sutton Coldfield
08418		West Coast Railway Company, Carnforth
08423	H011 14	PD Ports, Teesport, Grangetown, Middlesbrough
08441		Virgin Trains East Coast, Bounds Green Depot, London
08442		Arriva TrainCare, Eastleigh Depot, Hampshire
08445		Daventry International Railfreight Terminal, Crick
08447		John G Russell (Transport), Hillington, Glasgow
08460		RSS, Rye Farm, Wishaw, Sutton Coldfield
08484	CAPTAIN NATHANIEL DARELL	Bombardier Transportation, Derby Works
08485		West Coast Railway Company, Carnforth
08499	REDLIGHT	Colas Rail, Canton Depot, Cardiff
08500		Nemesis Rail, Burton-upon-Trent, Staffordshire
08502		GB Railfreight, Garston Car Terminal, Liverpool
08503		Barry Island Railway, Vale of Glamorgan
08511		Chasewater Light Railway, Brownhill, Staffordshire
08516		Arriva TrainCare, Barton Hill Depot, Bristol
08527		Barrow Hill Roundhouse, Chesterfield, Derbyshire
08536		LORAM, RTC Business Park, Derby
08507		Arlington Fleet Services, Eastleigh Works, Hampshire
08568	St. Rollox	Knorr-Bremse Rail Systems, Springburn Depot, Glasgow
08573		Bombardier Transportation, Ilford Works, London
08578		Quinton Rail Technology Centre, Long Marston, Warks
08580		Colne Valley Railway, Halstead, Essex

EX-BR MAIN LINE LOCOS IN INDUSTRIAL SERVICE 83

08588		Cemex UK, Washwood Heath, Birmingham
08593		RSS, Rye Farm, Wishaw, Sutton Coldfield
08598	H016 HERCULES	Chasewater Light Railway, Brownhills, Staffordshire
08600		AV Dawson, Ayrton Rail Terminal, Middlesbrough
08602	004	Bombardier Transportation, Derby Works
08613	H064	Celtic Energy, Onllwyn Coal & Distribution Centre, W Glamorgan
08622	H028 19	Hanson Cement, Ketton Cement Works, nr Stamford
08629	Wolverton	Knorr-Bremse Rail Systems, Wolverton Works, Milton Keynes
08630	CELSA 3	Celsa Steel UK, Tremorfa Steelworks, Cardiff
08643		Aggregate Industries, Merehead Rail Terminal
08648		Northern, Heaton Depot, Newcastle-upon-Tyne
08649	Bradwell	Knorr-Bremse Rail Systems, Wolverton Works, Milton Keynes
08650	ISLE OF GRAIN	Hanson Aggregates, Whatley Quarry, near Frome
08652		Hanson Aggregates, Whatley Quarry, near Frome
08653		Quinton Rail Technology Centre, Long Marston, Warks
08670		Virgin Trains East Coast, Bounds Green Depot, London
08676		Barrow Hill Roundhouse, Chesterfield, Derbyshire
08678	ARTILA	West Coast Railway Company, Carnforth
08682	Lionheart	Bombardier Transportation, Derby Works
08683		RSS, Rye Farm, Wishaw, Sutton Coldfield
08685		Barrow Hill Roundhouse, Chesterfield, Derbyshire
08699		Weardale Railway, Wolsingham, County Durham
08700		Bombardier Transportation, Ilford Works, London
08701		Quinton Rail Technology Centre, Long Marston, Warks
08704		Nemesis Rail, Burton-upon-Trent, Staffordshire
08709		Colne Valley Railway, Halstead, Essex
08711		Tees Yard *(awaiting collection by HNRC)*
08714		Crewe International Depot *(awaiting collection by HNRC)*
08730	The Caley	Knorr-Bremse Rail Systems, Springburn Depot, Glasgow
08738		Colne Valley Railway, Halstead, Essex
08743	Bryan Turner	SembCorp Utilities Teesside, Wilton, Middlesbrough
08750		Weardale Railway, Wolsingham, County Durham
08756		Tata Steel, Shotton Works, Deeside, Flintshire
08762		LORAM, RTC Business Park, Derby
08765		Barrow Hill Roundhouse, Chesterfield, Derbyshire
08774	ARTHUR VERNON DAWSON	AV Dawson, Ayrton Rail Terminal, Middlesbrough
08786		Barrow Hill Roundhouse, Chesterfield, Derbyshire
08787	"08296"	Hanson Aggregates, Machen Quarry, nr Newport
08802		RSS, Rye Farm, Wishaw, Sutton Coldfield
08807		AV Dawson, Ayrton Rail Terminal, Middlesbrough
08809	24	PD Ports, Teesport, Grangetown, Middlesbrough
08810	RICHARD J. WENHAM EASTLEIGH DEPOT	Arriva TrainCare, Eastleigh Depot, Hampshire
08818	MOLLY	Celsa Steel UK, Tremorfa Steelworks, Cardiff
08823	LIBBIE	Daventry International Railfreight Terminal, Crick
08824	IEMD 01	Barrow Hill Roundhouse, Chesterfield, Derbyshire
08834		Northern, Allerton Depot, Liverpool
08846	003	RSS, Rye Farm, Wishaw, Sutton Coldfield
08865		RSS, Rye Farm, Wishaw, Sutton Coldfield
08868		Arriva TrainCare, Crewe Depot, Cheshire

84 EX-BR MAIN LINE LOCOS IN INDUSTRIAL SERVICE

08870	H024	Weardale Railway, Wolsingham, County Durham
08871	H074	Tata Steel, Trostre Works, Llanelli, Carmarthenshire
08873		LH Group, Barton-under-Needwood, Staffordshire
08877		Barrow Hill Roundhouse, Chesterfield, Derbyshire
08885	H042 18	Weardale Railway, Wolsingham, County Durham
08892		Bombardier Transportation, Old Dalby Test Centre, Asfordby
08903	John W Antill	SembCorp Utilities Teesside, Wilton, Middlesbrough
08905		Hope Construction Materials, Hope Cement Works, Derbyshire
08912		AV Dawson, Ayrton Rail Terminal, Middlesbrough
08913		LH Group, Barton-under-Needwood, Staffordshire
08918		Nemesis Rail, Burton-upon-Trent, Staffordshire
08924	CELSA 2	Celsa Steel UK, Tremorfa Steelworks, Cardiff
08927	D4157	EMD, Roberts Road Depot, Doncaster
08933		Aggregate Industries, Merehead Rail Terminal
08936		Weardale Railway, Wolsingham, County Durham
08937	D4167	Bardon Aggregates, Meldon Quarry, near Okehampton
08939		Colne Valley Railway, Halstead, Essex
08943		Bombardier Transportation, Central Rivers Depot, Barton
08947		Hanson Aggregates, Whatley Quarry, near Frome
08956		Bombardier Transportation, Old Dalby Test Centre, Asfordby
08994		Nemesis Rail, Burton-upon-Trent, Staffordshire

Class 09

09006		Nemesis Rail, Burton-upon-Trent, Staffordshire
09007	D3671	London Overground, Willesden Depot, London
09014		Nemesis Rail, Burton-upon-Trent, Staffordshire
09022		Victoria Group, Port of Boston, Boston
09201		Hope Construction Materials, Hope Cement Works, Derbyshire
09204		Arriva TrainCare, Crewe Depot, Cheshire

Class 20

20056	81	Tata Steel, Appleby-Frodingham Works, Scunthorpe
20066	82	Hope Construction Materials, Hope Cement Works, Derbyshire
20110	D8110	Bury, East Lancashire Railway
20121		Barrow Hill Roundhouse, Chesterfield, Derbyshire
20166		Wensleydale Railway, Leeming Bar, North Yorkshire
20168	2 SIR GEORGE EARLE	Hope Construction Materials, Hope Cement Works, Derbyshire
20906	3	Hope Construction Materials, Hope Cement Works, Derbyshire

Class 47

47703	Wabtec Rail, Doncaster Works
47714	Bombardier Transportation, Old Dalby Test Centre, Asfordby

5. LOCOMOTIVES AWAITING DISPOSAL

Locomotives that are still extant but best classed as awaiting disposal are listed here.

Class 08

08783	European Metal Recycling, Kingsbury
08798	European Metal Recycling, Attercliffe
08872	European Metal Recycling, Attercliffe
08921	European Metal Recycling, Kingsbury

Class 09

09023	European Metal Recycling, Attercliffe
09107	European Metal Recycling, Kingsbury

Class 58

58012	Battlefield Line
58023	Battlefield Line

Class 66

66048	EMD, Longport Works

Class 86

86901	CF Booth, Rotherham
86902	CF Booth, Rotherham

6. LOCOMOTIVES EXPORTED FOR USE ABROAD

This section details former BR (plus privatisation era) diesel and electric locomotives that have been exported from the UK for use in industrial locations or by a main line operator abroad. Not included are locos that are "preserved" abroad, which are included in our "Preserved Locomotives of British Railways" publication. (S) denotes locomotives that are stored.

Number Other no./name Location

Class 03

D2xxx	Ferramento Pugliesse, Terlizzi, Bari, Italy

Class 04

D2289	Lonato SpA, Lonato Steelworks, Lonato, Brescia, Italy

Class 47

47375	92 70 00 47375-5	Continental Railway Solution, Hungary

Class 56

56101	0659 001-5	FLOYD, Hungary
56115	0659 002-3	FLOYD, Hungary
56117	0659 003-1	FLOYD, Hungary (S)

Class 58

58001		Axiom Rail, France, (S) Alizay
58004		Axiom Rail, France, (S) Alizay
58005		Axiom Rail, France, (S) Alizay
58006		Axiom Rail, France, (S) Alizay
58007		Axiom Rail, France, (S) Alizay
58009		Axiom Rail, France, (S) Alizay
58010		Axiom Rail, France, (S) Alizay
58011		Axiom Rail, France, (S) Alizay
58013		Axiom Rail, France, (S) Alizay
58015		Transfesa, Spain, Monforte del Cid, Alicante
58018		Axiom Rail, France, (S) Alizay
58020	L43	Transfesa, Spain, Monforte del Cid, Alicante
58021		Axiom Rail, France, (S) Alizay
58024	L42	Transfesa, Spain, Monforte del Cid, Alicante
58025		DB Schenker, Spain, (S) Albacete
58026		Axiom Rail, France, (S) Alizay
58027	L52	DB Schenker, Spain, (S) Albacete
58029	L44	Transfesa, Spain, Monforte del Cid, Alicante
58030	L46	Transfesa, Spain, Monforte del Cid, Alicante
58031	L45	Transfesa, Spain, Monforte del Cid, Alicante
58032		Axiom Rail, France, (S) Alizay
58033		Axiom Rail, France, (S) Alizay
58034		Axiom Rail, France, (S) Alizay

LOCOMOTIVES EXPORTED FOR USE ABROAD 87

58035		Axiom Rail, France, (S) Alizay
58036		Axiom Rail, France, (S) Alizay
58038		Axiom Rail, France, (S) Alizay
58039		Axiom Rail, France, (S) Alizay
58040		Axiom Rail, France, (S) Alizay
58041	L36	Transfesa, Spain, (S) Albacete
58042		Axiom Rail, France, (S) Alizay
58043	L37	Transfesa, Spain, Monforte del Cid, Alicante
58044		Axiom Rail, France, (S) Woippy, Metz
58046		Axiom Rail, France, (S) Alizay
58047	L51	Transfesa, Spain, Monforte del Cid, Alicante
58049		Axiom Rail, France, (S) Alizay
58050	L53	DB Schenker, Spain, (S) Albacete

Class 66

66010	Euro Cargo Rail, France	66205	Euro Cargo Rail, France
66022	Euro Cargo Rail, France	66208	Euro Cargo Rail, France
66026	Euro Cargo Rail, France	66209	Euro Cargo Rail, France
66028	Euro Cargo Rail, France	66210	Euro Cargo Rail, France
66029	Euro Cargo Rail, France	66211	Euro Cargo Rail, France
66032	Euro Cargo Rail, France	66212	Euro Cargo Rail, France
66033	Euro Cargo Rail, France	66214	Euro Cargo Rail, France
66036	Euro Cargo Rail, France	66215	Euro Cargo Rail, France
66038	Euro Cargo Rail, France	66216	Euro Cargo Rail, France
66042	Euro Cargo Rail, France	66217	Euro Cargo Rail, France
66045	Euro Cargo Rail, France	66218	Euro Cargo Rail, France
66049	Euro Cargo Rail, France	66219	Euro Cargo Rail, France
66052	Euro Cargo Rail, France	66220	DB Cargo Polska, Poland
66062	Euro Cargo Rail, France	66222	Euro Cargo Rail, France
66064	Euro Cargo Rail, France	66223	Euro Cargo Rail, France
66071	Euro Cargo Rail, France	66224	Euro Cargo Rail, France
66072	Euro Cargo Rail, France	66225	Euro Cargo Rail, France
66073	Euro Cargo Rail, France	66226	Euro Cargo Rail, France
66123	Euro Cargo Rail, France	66227	DB Cargo Polska, Poland
66146	DB Cargo Polska, Poland	66228	Euro Cargo Rail, France
66153	DB Cargo Polska, Poland	66229	Euro Cargo Rail, France
66157	DB Cargo Polska, Poland	66231	Euro Cargo Rail, France
66159	DB Cargo Polska, Poland	66233	Euro Cargo Rail, France
66163	DB Cargo Polska, Poland	66234	Euro Cargo Rail, France
66166	DB Cargo Polska, Poland	66235	Euro Cargo Rail, France
66173	DB Cargo Polska, Poland	66236	Euro Cargo Rail, France
66178	DB Cargo Polska, Poland	66237	DB Cargo Polska, Poland
66179	Euro Cargo Rail, France	66239	Euro Cargo Rail, France
66180	DB Cargo Polska, Poland	66240	Euro Cargo Rail, France
66189	DB Cargo Polska, Poland	66241	Euro Cargo Rail, France
66190	Euro Cargo Rail, France	66242	Euro Cargo Rail, France
66191	Euro Cargo Rail, France	66243	Euro Cargo Rail, France
66195	Euro Cargo Rail, France	66244	Euro Cargo Rail, France
66196	DB Cargo Polska, Poland	66245	Euro Cargo Rail, France
66202	Euro Cargo Rail, France	66246	Euro Cargo Rail, France
66203	Euro Cargo Rail, France	66247	Euro Cargo Rail, France

LOCOMOTIVES EXPORTED FOR USE ABROAD

66248	DB Cargo Polska, Poland	66583	66010 Freightliner, Poland
66249	Euro Cargo Rail, France	66584	66011 Freightliner, Poland
66411	66013 Freightliner, Poland	66586	66008 Freightliner, Poland
66412	66015 Freightliner, Poland	66608	66603 Freightliner, Poland
66417	66014 Freightliner, Poland	66609	66604 Freightliner, Poland
66527	66016 Freightliner, Poland	66611	66605 Freightliner, Poland
66530	66017 Freightliner, Poland	66612	66606 Freightliner, Poland
66535	66018 Freightliner, Poland	66624	66602 Freightliner, Poland
66582	66009 Freightliner, Poland	66625	66601 Freightliner, Poland

Class 86

86213	Lancashire Witch	Bulmarket, Bulgaria
86215	91 55 0450 005-8	FLOYD, Hungary
86217	91 55 0450 006-6	FLOYD, Hungary
86218	91 55 0450 004-1	FLOYD, Hungary
86228	91 55 0450 007-4	FLOYD, Hungary
86231		Bulmarket, Bulgaria (S)
86232	91 55 0450 003-3	FLOYD, Hungary
86233		Bulmarket, Bulgaria (S)
86234		Bulmarket, Bulgaria (S)
86235		Bulmarket, Bulgaria
86242	91 55 0450 008-2	FLOYD, Hungary
86248	91 55 0450 001-7	FLOYD, Hungary
86250	91 55 0450 002-5	FLOYD, Hungary
86424	91 55 0450 009-0	FLOYD, Hungary (S)
86701	Orion	Bulmarket, Bulgaria
86702	Cassiopeia	Bulmarket, Bulgaria

Class 87

87003	87003-0	BZK, Bulgaria
87004	87004-8 Britannia	BZK, Bulgaria
87006	87006-3	BZK, Bulgaria
87007	87007-1	BZK, Bulgaria
87008	87008-9	BZK, Bulgaria (S)
87009		Bulmarket, Bulgaria
87010	87010-5	BZK, Bulgaria
87012	87012-1	BZK, Bulgaria
87013	87013-9	BZK, Bulgaria
87014	87014-7	BZK, Bulgaria (S)
87017	Iron Duke	Bulmarket, Bulgaria
87019	87019-6	BZK, Bulgaria
87020	87020-4	BZK, Bulgaria
87022	87022-0	BZK, Bulgaria
87023	Velocity	Bulmarket, Bulgaria
87025		Bulmarket, Bulgaria
87026	87026-1	BZK, Bulgaria
87028	87028-7	BZK, Bulgaria
87029	87029-5	BZK, Bulgaria
87033	87033-7	BZK, Bulgaria
87034	87034-5	BZK, Bulgaria

LOCOMOTIVES EXPORTED FOR USE ABROAD

Class 92

92001	91 53 0472 002-1 Mircea Eliade	DB Cargo, Romania
92002	H.G. Wells	DB Cargo, Romania
92003	Beethoven	DB Cargo, Romania
92005	Mozart	DB Cargo, Romania
92012	91 53 0472 001-3 Mihai Eminescu	DB Cargo, Romania
92024	J.S. Bach	DB Cargo, Romania
92025	Oscar Wilde	DB Cargo, Bulgaria
92026	Britten	DB Cargo, Romania
92027	George Eliot	DB Cargo, Bulgaria
92030	Ashford	DB Cargo, Bulgaria
92034	Kipling	DB Cargo, Bulgaria
92039	Johann Strauss	DB Cargo, Romania

7. CODES

7.1. LIVERY CODES

Livery codes are used to denote the various liveries carried. It is impossible to list every livery variation which currently exists, in particular items ignored for this publication include:

- Minor colour variations.
- Omission of logos.
- All numbering, lettering and brandings.

Descriptions quoted are thus a general guide only. Logos as appropriate for each livery are normally deemed to be carried. The colour of the lower half of the bodyside is stated first.

- **AB** Arriva Trains Wales/Welsh Government sponsored dark blue.
- **AI** Aggregate Industries (green, light grey & blue).
- **AL** Advertising/promotional livery (see class heading for details).
- **AR** Anglia Railways (turquoise blue with a white stripe).
- **AZ** Advenza Freight (deep blue with green Advenza brandings).
- **B** BR blue.
- **BL** BR Revised blue with yellow cabs, grey roof, large numbers & logo.
- **CA** Caledonian Sleeper (dark blue).
- **CD** Cotswold Rail (silver with blue & red logo).
- **CE** BR Civil Engineers (yellow & grey with black cab doors & window surrounds).
- **CM** Chiltern Mainline loco-hauled (two-tone grey & silver with blue stripes).
- **CS** Colas Rail (yellow, orange & black).
- **CU** Corus (silver with red logo).
- **DB** DB Cargo (Deutsche Bahn red with grey roof and solebar).
- **DC** Devon & Cornwall Railways (metallic silver).
- **DG** BR Departmental (dark grey with black cab doors & window surrounds).
- **DI** New DRS {Class 68 style} (deep blue & aquamarine with large compass logo).
- **DR** Direct Rail Services (dark blue with light blue or dark grey roof).
- **DS** Revised Direct Rail Services (dark blue, light blue & green. "Compass" logo).
- **E** English Welsh & Scottish Railway (maroon bodyside & roof with a broad gold bodyside band).
- **EB** Eurotunnel (two-tone grey with a broad blue stripe).
- **EG** "EWS grey" (as **F** but with large yellow & red EWS logo).
- **EP** European Passenger Services (two-tone grey with dark blue roof).
- **EX** Europhoenix (silver, blue & red).
- **F** BR Trainload Freight (two-tone grey with black cab doors & window surrounds. Various logos).
- **FA** Fastline Freight (grey & black with white & orange stripes).
- **FB** First Group dark blue.
- **FE** Railfreight Distribution International (two tone-grey with black cab doors & dark blue roof).
- **FER** Fertis (light grey with a dark grey roof & solebar).

CODES

- **FF** Freightliner grey (two-tone grey with black cab doors & window surrounds. Freightliner logo).
- **FH** Revised Freightliner {PowerHaul} (dark green with yellow ends & a grey stripe/buffer beam).
- **FL** Freightliner (dark green with yellow cabs).
- **FO** BR Freightliner (grey bodysides, yellow cabs & red lower bodyside stripe, large BR logo).
- **FR** Fragonset Railways (black with silver roof & a red bodyside band lined out in white).
- **FS** First Group (indigo blue with pink & white stripes).
- **FY** Foster Yeoman (blue & silver. Cast numberplates).
- **G** BR Green (plain green, with white stripe on main line locomotives).
- **GA** Abellio Greater Anglia (white with a black stripe).
- **GB** GB Railfreight (blue with orange cantrail & solebar stripes, orange cabs).
- **GC** Grand Central (all over black with an orange stripe).
- **GG** BR green (two-tone green).
- **GIF** GIF (Spain) light blue with a dark blue band.
- **GL** First Great Western locomotives (green with a gold stripe (no gold stripe on shunters)).
- **GW** Great Western Railway (TOC) dark green.
- **GY** Eurotunnel (grey & yellow).
- **HA** Hanson Quarry Products (dark blue/silver with oxide red roof).
- **HN** Harry Needle Railroad Company (orange with a black roof and solebar).
- **IC** BR InterCity (dark grey/white/red/white).
- **K** Black.
- **LH** BR Loadhaul (black with orange cabsides).
- **LM** London Midland (white/grey & green with broad black stripe around the windows).
- **M** Maroon.
- **ML** BR Mainline Freight (aircraft blue with a silver stripe).
- **N** BR Network SouthEast (white & blue with red lower bodyside stripe, grey solebar & cab ends).
- **O** Non-standard (see class heading for details).
- **PC** Pullman Car Company (umber & cream with gold lettering lined out in gold).
- **RB** Riviera Trains Oxford blue.
- **RG** BR Parcels (dark grey & red).
- **RS** RMS Locotec blue.
- **RX** Rail Express Systems (dark grey & red with or without blue markings).
- **RZ** Royal Train revised (plain claret, no lining).
- **SD** South West Trains outer suburban {Class 450 style} (deep blue, orange & red).
- **SL** Silverlink (indigo blue with white stripe, green lower body & yellow doors).
- **SN** Southern (white & dark green with light green semi-circles at one end of each vehicle. Light grey band at solebar level).
- **SR** ScotRail – Scotland's Railways (dark blue with Scottish Saltire flag & white/light blue flashes).
- **ST** Stagecoach (blue with red cabs).
- **TT** Transmart Trains (all over green).
- **V** Virgin Trains (red with black doors extending into bodysides, three white lower bodyside stripes).
- **VE** Virgin Trains East Coast (red & white with black window surrounds).

VN	Belmond Northern Belle (crimson lake & cream lined out in gold).
VP	Virgin Trains shunters (black with a large black & white chequered flag on the bodyside).
WA	Wabtec Rail (black).
WC	West Coast Railway Company maroon.
XC	CrossCountry (two-tone silver with deep crimson ends and pink doors).
Y	Network Rail yellow.

7.2. OWNER CODES

Locomotives and rolling stock are owned by various companies and private owners and are allotted codes as follows:

20	Class 20189
37	Scottish Thirty-Seven Group
40	Class 40 Preservation Society
47	Stratford 47 Group
50	Class 50 Alliance
56	Class 56 Locomotives
70	7029 Clun Castle
71	71A Locomotives
2L	Class Twenty Locomotives
A	Angel Trains
AF	Arlington Fleet Services
AI	Aggregate Industries
AM	Alstom
AV	Arriva UK Trains
BA	British American Railway Services
BN	Beacon Rail
CS	Colas Rail
DB	DB Cargo UK
DP	Deltic Preservation Society
DR	Direct Rail Services
DT	The Diesel Traction Group
E	Eversholt Rail (UK)
EL	Electric Traction Limited
EM	East Midlands Trains
EP	Europhoenix
ET	Eurotunnel
EU	Eurostar International
FG	First Group
FL	Freightliner
GB	GB Railfreight
GW	Great Western Railway (assets of the Greater Western franchise)
HA	Hanson UK
HJ	Howard Johnston
HN	Harry Needle Railroad Company
LF	Lombard Finance
LO	LORAM
LM	London Midland

CODES

LS	Locomotive Services
MQ	Macquarie Group
MW	Martin Walker
NB	Neil Boden
NM	National Museum of Science & Industry
NR	Network Rail
NS	Nemesis Rail
NY	North Yorkshire Moors Railway Enterprises
P	Porterbrook Leasing Company
PP	Peter Pan Locomotive Company
RL	Rail Management Services (trading as RMS Locotec)
RO	Rail Operations Group
SP	The Scottish Railway Preservation Society
TT	Transmart Trains
UR	UK Rail Leasing
WA	Wabtec Rail Group
WC	West Coast Railway Company

7.3. LOCOMOTIVE POOL CODES

Locomotives are split into operational groups ("pools") for diagramming and maintenance purposes. The codes used to denote these pools are shown in this publication.

ATLO	Alstom Class 08.
AWCA	West Coast Railway Company operational locomotives.
AWCX	West Coast Railway Company stored locomotives.
CFOL	Class 50 Operations locomotives.
COFS	Colas Rail Classes 47 & 56.
COLO	Colas Rail Classes 60, 66 & 70.
COLS	Colas Rail stored locomotives.
COTS	Colas Rail Class 37.
DFGH	Freightliner Heavy Haul Class 70.
DFGI	Freightliner Intermodal Class 70.
DFHG	Freightliner Heavy Haul low emission Class 66.
DFHH	Freightliner Heavy Haul Class 66.
DFHJ	Freightliner Heavy Haul Class 66. Restricted use.
DFIM	Freightliner Intermodal Class 66.
DFIN	Freightliner Intermodal low emission Class 66.
DFLC	Freightliner Intermodal Class 90.
DFLH	Freightliner Heavy Haul Class 47.
DFLS	Freightliner Class 08.
DFNC	Freightliner Intermodal Class 86/6.
DHLT	Freightliner locomotives awaiting maintenance/repair/disposal.
EFOO	Great Western Railway Class 57.
EFPC	Great Western Railway 43.
EFSH	Great Western Railway 08.
EHPC	CrossCountry Class 43.
EJLO	London Midland Class 08.
ELRD	East Lancashire Railway-based main line registered locomotives.

CODES

EMPC	East Midlands Trains Class 43.
EMSL	East Midlands Trains Class 08.
EPEX	Europhoenix locomotives for export.
EPUK	Europhoenix UK locomotives.
GBBR	GB Railfreight Class 73 for possible rebuilding.
GBBT	GB Railfreight Class 66. Large fuel tanks.
GBCH	GB Railfreight Class 86/87.
GBCS	GB Railfreight Class 73/9. Caledonian Sleeper.
GBEB	GB Railfreight Class 66. Ex-European, large fuel tanks.
GBED	GB Railfreight Class 73.
GBEE	GB Railfreight Class 20. On hire from Harry Needle/Class 20189.
GBEL	GB Railfreight Class 66. New build, small fuel tanks.
GBET	GB Railfreight Class 92. Stored locomotives.
GBFM	GB Railfreight Class 66. RETB fitted.
GBHN	GB Railfreight Class 47. Hired from HNRC.
GBLT	GB Railfreight Class 66. Small fuel tanks.
GBNB	GB Railfreight Class 66. New build.
GBNR	GB Railfreight Class 73/9. Network Rail contracts.
GBSL	GB Railfreight Class 92. Caledonian Sleeper.
GBST	GB Railfreight Class 92. Caledonian Sleeper & Channel Tunnel.
GBWM	GB Railfreight Class 08/09.
GBYH	GB Railfreight Class 59.
GCHP	Grand Central Class 43.
GPSS	Eurostar (UK) Class 08.
GROG	Rail Operations Group operational locomotives.
HBSH	Wabtec hire shunting locomotives.
HNRL	Harry Needle Railroad Company hire locomotives.
HNRS	Harry Needle Railroad Company stored locomotives.
HTLX	British American Railway Services locomotives.
HYWD	South West Trains Class 73.
IANA	Abellio Greater Anglia Class 90.
IECA	Virgin Trains East Coast Class 91.
IECP	Virgin Trains East Coast Class 43.
MBDL	Non TOC-owned diesel locomotives.
MBED	Non TOC-owned electro-diesel locomotives.
MBEL	Non TOC-owned electric locomotives.
MOLO	Class 20189 Ltd Class 20.
MRSO	RMS Locotec Class 08.
NRLO	Nemesis Rail locomotives.
QADD	Network Rail locomotives.
QCAR	Network Rail New Measurement Train Class 43.
QETS	Network Rail Class 37.
RFSH	Wabtec Rail locomotives.
RVLO	LORAM locomotives.
UKRL	UK Rail Leasing. Operational locomotives.
UKRM	UK Rail Leasing. Locomotives for overhaul.
UKRS	UK Rail Leasing. Stored locomotives.
WAAC	DB Cargo Class 67.
WABC	DB Cargo Class 67. RETB fitted.
WAWC	DB Cargo Class 67 for hire to Arriva Trains Wales.
WBAE	DB Cargo Class 66. Locomotives fitted with "stop-start" technology.

CODES

WBAR	DB Cargo Class 66. Fitted with remote monitoring equipment.
WBAT	DB Cargo Class 66.
WBBE	DB Cargo Class 66. RETB fitted and fitted with "stop-start" technology.
WBBT	DB Cargo Class 66. RETB fitted.
WBLE	DB Cargo Class 66. Dedicated locomotives for Lickey Incline banking duties. Fitted with "stop-start" technology.
WBLT	DB Cargo Class 66. Dedicated locomotives for Lickey Incline banking duties.
WBTT	DB Cargo Class 66. Fitted with tripcocks.
WCAT	DB Cargo Class 60.
WCBT	DB Cargo Class 60. Extended-range fuel tanks.
WDAM	DB Cargo Class 59.
WEAC	DB Cargo Class 90.
WFBC	DB Cargo Class 92 with commissioned TVM430 cab signalling equipment for use on High Speed 1.
WGEA	DB Cargo locomotives for export.
WQAA	DB Cargo stored locomotives Group 1A (short-term maintenance).
WQAB	DB Cargo stored locomotives Group 1B.
WQBA	DB Cargo stored locomotives Group 2 (unserviceable).
WQCA	DB Cargo stored locomotives Group 3 (unserviceable).
WQDA	DB Cargo stored locomotives Group 4 (awaiting disposal).
WSGC	DB Cargo Class 09. GSMR fitted.
WSRC	DB Cargo Class 08. Remote control fitted.
WSSC	DB Cargo Class 08.
XHAC	Direct Rail Services Classes 37/4 & 57/3.
XHCC	Direct Rail Services Class 37/4. Cumbrian Coast passenger.
XHCE	Direct Rail Services Class 68 for hire to Chiltern Railways.
XHCK	Direct Rail Services Class 57/0.
XHHP	Direct Rail Services locomotives – holding pool.
XHIM	Direct Rail Services locomotives – Intermodal traffic.
XHNC	Direct Rail Services locomotives – nuclear traffic/general.
XHSS	Direct Rail Services stored locomotives.
XHVE	Direct Rail Services Class 68.
XHVT	Direct Rail Services Class 57/3 for hire to Virgin Trains West Coast.
XYPA	Mendip Rail Class 59/1.
XYPO	Mendip Rail Class 59/0.

7.4. ALLOCATION & LOCATION CODES

Allocation codes are used in this publication to denote the normal maintenance base ("depots") of each operational locomotive. However, maintenance may be carried out at other locations and also by mobile teams. The designation (S) denotes stored.

Code	Location	Depot Operator
BA	Basford Hall Yard (Crewe)	Freightliner
BH	Barrow Hill (Chesterfield)	Barrow Hill Engine Shed Society
BL	Shackerstone, Battlefield Line	*Storage location only*
BM	Bournemouth	South West Trains
BN	Bounds Green (London)	Virgin Trains East Coast

CODES

Code	Location	Operator
BO	Bo'ness (West Lothian)	The Bo'ness & Kinneil Railway
BQ	Bury (Greater Manchester)	East Lancashire Railway Trust
BU	Burton-upon-Trent	Nemesis Rail
CE	Crewe International	DB Cargo UK
CL	Crewe LNWR Heritage	LNWR Heritage Company
CO	Coquelles (France)	Eurotunnel
CP	Crewe Arriva TrainCare	Arriva TrainCare
CR	Crewe Gresty Bridge	Direct Rail Services
CS	Carnforth	West Coast Railway Company
EC	Edinburgh Craigentinny	Virgin Trains East Coast
HT	Heaton (Newcastle)	Northern
KM	Carlisle Kingmoor	Direct Rail Services
KR	Kidderminster	Severn Valley Railway
LA	Laira (Plymouth)	Great Western Railway
LB	Loughborough Works	Brush Traction
LD	Leeds Midland Road	Freightliner Engineering
LE	Landore (Swansea)	Great Western Railway
LM	Long Marston (Warwickshire)	Quinton Rail Technology Centre
LR	Leicester	UK Rail Leasing
LW	MoD Longtown	*Storage location only*
MD	Merehead	Mendip Rail
NC	Norwich Crown Point	Abellio Greater Anglia
NL	Neville Hill (Leeds)	East Midlands Trains/Northern
NY	Grosmont (North Yorkshire)	North Yorkshire Moors Railway Enterprises
OO	Old Oak Common HST	Great Western Railway
PG	Peterborough GBRf	GB Railfreight
RR	Doncaster Robert's Road	ElectroMotive Diesel Services
RU	Rugby	Colas Rail
SE	St Leonards (Hastings)	St Leonards Railway Engineering
SL	Stewarts Lane (London)	Govia Thameslink Railway/Belmond
SK	Swanwick Junction (Derbyshire)	Midland Railway Enterprises
TM	Tyseley Locomotive Works	Birmingham Railway Museum
TO	Toton (Nottinghamshire)	DB Cargo UK
WH	Washwood Heath (Birmingham)	Boden Rail Engineering/RMS Locotec
WN	Willesden (London)	London Overground
WO	Wolsingham, Weardale Railway	RMS Locotec
YK	National Railway Museum (York)	National Museum of Science & Industry
ZA	RTC Business Park (Derby)	LORAM
ZB	Doncaster Works	Wabtec Rail
ZC	Crewe Works	Bombardier Transportation UK
ZD	Derby Works	Bombardier Transportation UK
ZG	Eastleigh Works	Arlington Fleet Services
ZH	Springburn Depot (Glasgow)	Knorr-Bremse Rail Systems (UK)
ZI	Ilford Works	Bombardier Transportation UK
ZJ	Stoke-on-Trent Works	Axiom Rail (Stoke)
ZK	Kilmarnock Works	Wabtec Rail Scotland
ZN	Wolverton Works	Knorr-Bremse Rail Systems (UK)
ZR	York (Holgate Works)	Network Rail